TALES FROM THE ETHER

An Anthology of Short Form: Poetry, Fiction and Non-Fiction.

Warwick Writers

Orange Petal Press

Copyright © 2021 Each writer who has contributed a piece to this anthology retain their own copyright.

All rights reserved

The characters and events portrayed in this book are fictitious. Any similarity to real persons, living or dead, is coincidental and not intended by the author.

No part of this book may be reproduced, or stored in a retrieval system, or transmitted in any form or by any means, electronic, mechanical, photocopying, recording, or otherwise, without express written permission of the publisher.

ISBN-13: 9798723397491
ISBN-10: 1477123456

Cover design by: Art Painter
Library of Congress Control Number: 2018675309
Printed in the United States of America

Dedicated to all the wonderful writers whose work has been included in the anthology.

CONTENTS

Title Page
Copyright
Dedication
INTRODUCTION
Tales from the Ether   1
1. Things Are Not What They Seem   2
I Thought We Were Millionaires   3
Growth   5
Pier   10
Till Death Do Us Part   19
2. Outsiders   23
After A Party   24
The Orphanage   25
Bordering   30
Restaurant of the Heart   32
3. We Can Be Heroes   36
Life Lessons From Lobsters   37
I Am Katherine Margaret Hall, The Wonder Woman   40
False God   42
4. Villains   44
Graveyard Guardian   45

What We See	48
Misplaced	52
Soap	54
5. Girlhood	60
On Reading Miss Brill	61
50-East	63
An Ode To Puberty	69
6. Places I Have Loved	76
The First Footing	77
The Doctor's House	83
7. Age Cannot Wither Us	88
For All Time	89
Bullets in the Face	95
DNR	98
Smoke Spirit	99
8. Spring And Port Wine	102
Food Bank	103
For All Time, Dear Friend	110
9. Dreams And Nightmares	116
One Day	117
The Craving	118
Snap Alley	122
Circles	126
10. Meet The Writers	130
Bios	131
Epilogue	139
Acknowledgement	141

INTRODUCTION

Tales from the Ether is an anthology that celebrates insightful and poignant short pieces of fiction, non-fiction, and poetry by emerging writers. Some of our writers are starting out; others are winning awards for their writing. Many of our writers come from under-represented groups, which is something we're proud of. And although English is their medium, our writers are international, hailing from Australia, India, Indonesia, Italy, UK, and US.

How have we gathered this diverse collection of writing? *Tales from the Ether* is borne out of *Flash Fix*, an award-winning radio show on RAW 1251AM. With the show, we wanted to bring a satisfying dose of short form storytelling straight into the homes of our listeners. When lockdowns started amidst the Covid-19 pandemic *Flash Fix* continued to keep us all company as a podcast.

While sharing the same spirit of the podcast, *Tales from the Ether* emerges from our desire to present these stories in book form. We hope this is where we can reach new readers and audiences.

We hope you enjoy these tales as much as we've enjoyed putting them together.

orangepetalpress.com

orangepetalpress@gmail.com

TALES FROM THE ETHER

1. THINGS ARE NOT WHAT THEY SEEM

I THOUGHT WE WERE MILLIONAIRES

Abigail Penny

I thought we were millionaires
   because we had a wooden table
   I thought we had been good
when we were given cereal for lunch
I thought my mum was fancy
which was why she always dieted
I thought we were spoilt
because my brothers and I slept in the big bed
while mum and dad slept by the door.
I thought dad was too strict
when he said we couldn't play in the streets after dark
We were the good family
the one with mum *and* dad
we don't go into other people's homes
and make a mess and fuss
we come right home after school
don't play in the streets after dark.

But the wooden table was left on the streets
dad stole it before the council could take it

and no matter how good or bad we were
cereal was all we had to eat.
We never visited our friends
because mum and dad couldn't risk
their sons picking up bad habits
that would rob them of a future
My mother never ate
because she couldn't afford for us to starve
she sat with a smile I knew was sad,
and held her gurgling stomach by the door
waiting for dad to come home
They'd lock my brothers and I in the big bedroom
and they'd sleep by the door
with a knife under the cushion
and never wake up rested
I'm older now, an office manager
and I work with a lot of people
Some of them drive Audis
and buy everyone Moet at the races
some of them have children
who don't know the word no.
I live in a two bedroom flat
I can drink all the milk I want
I don't have to fix my shoelaces when they break
I know more than anyone I work with
and anyone in the world
what it is to be a millionaire
because we were millionaires:
We ate our meals on a wooden table
our parents came home every night
and we never played in the streets
after dark.

GROWTH

Cheryl Powell

Published in The Mechanics Institute Review 2018

She held the scalpel up to the light and checked its blade. The edge was laser sharp, and this was good, since quick clean cuts were the most painless, severing nerve endings before they could react.

Six scalpels ranging in size lay on the worktop beside the bath, and other surgical equipment: antimicrobial scrub, tweezers, swabs of cotton wool, wound dressings, surgical mask and a box of blue latex gloves.

She had nothing to lose. The kids had grown up and left home.

There was just the two of them now. She listened to the low rumble of planes taking off and landing at the airport nearby, passengers on their way to Spain, or India, or who knows where. Single travellers, trying to find themselves; women like her, perhaps, who had already had their surgery.

So she'd chosen a night when she wouldn't be disturbed, when he would be watching football downstairs, hand clutching the remote. She'd scoured the bathroom, put out white towels for afterwards, ice packs for the pain, and a new bottle of Jack Daniel's.

The lighting in the bathroom was as good as any operating theatre, brilliant white and shadowless. She wasted no time stripping off her clothes, stepping into the bath and pulling on the blue latex gloves. Her breathing laboured with the effort, the heaviness on her chest; the tightness in her ribcage had become unbearable lately. She was suffocating.

She would rid herself of this burden, of him, or die in the attempt.

The growth had spread. Facing the mirror above the sink, running blue fingers over her body, she could see that its mass now stretched from the top of her hip to below her knee. Over the years it had put out tentacles that twisted around her thighs and across her ribs: light scars at first, but now more bloated as they filled with blood and fluid, growing thicker and more prickly.

She secured the surgical mask over her face, carefully poured the brown antimicrobial scrub over her body. Taking the scalpel, she put her right foot on the edge of the bath. She would start on the flesh-like feelers just below her knee. Here the strands of growth looked just like calloused skin, waxy yellow and hardened. She was able to slice through it quite painlessly, prising it away from the new tissue underneath, peeling it back to the top of her kneecap. She breathed deeply, the mask inflating and deflating along its folds and she felt the heat and stale air building inside it, but she felt braver now she'd made a start.

Next she attacked the fronds just below her breastbone, gouging at the tiny barbs embedded in her flesh, her lungs so desperate for air she had to push the mask up into her hair.

She couldn't go on. The pain was too much.

He'd always said she'd never do it, that she didn't have the courage. That she was pathetic. Was this true? The reflection in the mirror wasn't her, at least not how she remembered herself. This body was overweight and flabby, the face fallen in on itself, and yet when she moved, the creature in the mirror moved, too; when she raised a hand, it raised a hand. And the growth was unmistakably hers, its lumpy terrain, craggy in some parts, smooth in others, mottled red-purple at its centre. She pulled the mask back into place, reached for an ice pack and held it to her outer thigh.

Looking back, she should have nipped the whole thing in the bud. A small pink lump on her right hip, like a solid blister, totally painless. But later it began to itch and when she looked more closely it had thick black hairs, like the legs of a tick, burrowed deep into her skin, and she had been horrified and too frightened to seek help.

Years later and the growth had intensified its stranglehold and become inflamed. She would scratch until she was too hot and short of breath, clawing at her flesh until she bled. It had got so bulky it chafed constantly. She had exchanged her fitted work suits for looser skirts and blousy jackets and felt relieved when they took her off reception to help in the back office.

She grabbed the scalpel again, took a slug of whisky, and probed the area around her stomach. Here, the growth was softer, and more vibrant, with beads and globules of fluid moving under the skin, like mineral oil inside a lava lamp. She made an incision and cried out. The pain was severe and her flesh sprang bright with blood. She seized the shower head and rinsed. A network of suckers tunnelled deep inside. She gritted her teeth and pushed the blade further, through the fatty layer and the tissue beyond, clamping down on a scream.

The growth had blighted her life. She never left the house. The reception girls still asked her on nights out, even though she no longer worked there, but he was never keen. Said they only invited her to talk about her afterwards. So, she always made an excuse, knowing that if she went she would only find a dark corner, invisible in the shapeless dress he'd chosen for her, conscious that, underneath, the growth would throb and tighten and everybody would know of her disfigurement.

She'd telephoned a hotline once. They told her she had to be strong.

Yes, she must be strong.

Swallowing more whisky, straight from the bottle, she pressed an ice pack to her hip. This is where the growth was most deeply embedded, locked in with its parasitic suckers, blind feelers groping into her cells. She threw off the surgical mask, snatched up a flannel and stuffed it into her mouth. Then she took the largest scalpel and opened up her hip, slicing away the flesh until the blood obscured her work and she had to press on more ice and her body began to judder with shock and the growth hung down, convulsing, folded over itself, clinging on by a few tough tendrils. Frantically, she hacked away, knowing she could easily die, bleed to death, but she was desperate to be rid of it.

The growth slithered into the bath, coiled into a ball, quaking and twitching, sliding in its own muck.

The bleeding stopped. She ran her fingers over where the growth had been. At last she was free of it. Already her flesh was beginning to heal, scabbing over, still sore and weeping at the centre but, as she showered off the blood, she saw it was a clean amputation. In time, she thought, it would heal completely, though there would always be deep scars and a permanent cavity at her hip.

She cleaned and dressed the worst of the wounds and stepped out of the bath, pulling a clean white towel around her. The growth shuddered, great awful spasms as it floundered in the bath, heaving, as though drawing itself together, pulling in its tentacles, amassing. And, as she stared, the growth lengthened and took shape: limbs and torso that looked familiar, the lines of a face she knew, and for a moment her breathing faltered, the old pull on her heart. Those eyes. The way they looked at her, eyes she knew so well but now with a different light in them. It spoke.

"I never thought you'd do it."

"I had to," is all she could say, and the tears fell. "I couldn't go on anymore. I'm sorry."

And he nodded, his mouth working, grimacing, as though in pain, and she felt the eternal throb at her hip where he had been cut away.

She had wanted this separation for such a long time, but as he eased away from her, backing off, she understood something else. That he had craved it more.

PIER

Benjamin Waller

Nathaniel walks along the beach, where he and Clare once walked and they'd made lines of endless play with language. Now he is joined only by sand, a blank page rescued from the surf, the ink run, unreadable, and ruined. The light rain washes him clean, at least for a time. Today, whilst looking for something else, he had found a letter in an old cardboard box. Something else because her relatives were pestering him for documents he had forgotten about, wills and wishes Clara may have written down, promises as to who could have what should the end arrive unexpectedly. Promises that she may well have forgotten about too.

He'd also dug out a six-by-four photograph of them together, on the beach here, big gloves wrapped around paper cups of steaming mulled wine, smiles framed by bobble hats and heavy winter coats, both looking so much younger. His smile was natural, less tight, he thought, so much more at ease. The gloss finish of the old print was slightly scratched, and he placed his own thumb over a chalky and powdery thumbprint impressed into the corner of the photograph, across a whorl smaller and thinner than his, almost certainly hers.

Nathaniel looks out at the sea, and when he closes his eyes, he sees Clare as he saw her that final day. Holding the cold hand in his,

Nathanial wished he could warm the heavy fingers back to life. He pushed loose and wild dyed dark hair back over her eyes and across her right ear, fixing it in place with a hair clip. He kissed her embalmed lips, cold and perfect, as lived in as cracked porcelain, as repaired as *Kintsugi*. The last meeting before that, at the wedding of a mutual friend, the last time they had hugged and said goodbye, they had inadvertently said farewell. That day he again regretted leaving her, and the way he left, but could not say so, to himself or anyone else. The moment they parted the air around him felt tangibly thinner without her, emptier and incomplete.

Words shimmer across the sea, love in phrases and nouns and verbs. They fly, flow and dart and craw craw to each other. He is in a liminal place, before the old world has died and the new world formed, the ebbing of the last tide before the sea arranges the mindscape anew: bottles with messages, endless plastic ephemera in every colour, and rust patterns in the ripples of the sand suggest that something once rested here, maybe a hulk of a past place they shared, and cargo that sits unseen beneath the waves, maybe her hair clip, maybe the small clasp of a necklace.

An ancient port by the old sea wall is now a sea-henge of rotting oak posts, mud flats and hulls of fishing boats that are cracked open wide to the air, rivets expelled, port and seaboard no longer parallel. He walks past lobster pots stacked high, plastic lures in industrial blue, past the untested concrete cubes of tank traps, the word-made-solid defiance sunk here to repel or at least slow landings in the last war, boundary markers of the ever-changing edge. Away from the harbour, a boat yields to the growing pitch and the yaw, the swell and swallow of the sea. The flash of the lighthouse passes across the waves and hits the deck. The distant and unknown captain of the craft is bathed in both the lamplight and last sunlight of the day, a light that forms a band of copper on the vanishing point of sky and sea, a light that is mirrored and held in the back of Nathaniel's eye.

Some of Clare's ashes floated on the waves, and Nathaniel wonders if they were supposed to have a permit for this kind of thing. God only knows why she wanted to be scattered at sea.

She'd never mentioned it to him. A couple of huge sharp-eyed seagulls land in the water, and pick at the ash, realise it is inedible (although could have been otherwise if prepared differently) and fly off.

Nathaniel nods to himself in the glass of the window of the railway ticket office, checks his hair, as Clare's almost grown-up children stroll around him in circles, waiting for direction. He doesn't linger for goodbyes, so quickly and discreetly bids farewell to Jack and Gail and walks around the corner to a table in the café, where he shoos away the pigeons that fill every surface in this station with filth. Carrier pigeons use magnetic fields, and the sun, and memory, and route themselves to where they want to return. The children will do much the same, but with sophisticated handheld tools and more considered defecation, probably. Someone once said technology is stuff that doesn't work yet. Beyond the station, the sky is a dirty grey and purple waterfall, refilling the sea so tomorrow all would be possible again.

Jack is open faced but ruddy cheeked, wearing a red and white tracksuit top, open to the waist, hiding the stomach that sags within the white t-shirt beneath like a partly filled sandbag. His white trainers are seeping seawater that forms pools wherever he stands. He's gone, he's gone, Jack said, shifting his weight from foot to foot. Gail is staring past Jack, into the street outside. Her fingers wrap and tousle the straightened black hair that sits like seaweed around an overpainted face, and glances back towards the platform that is a blur of people and bags, signs and symbols and sandwiches, all coerced and conducted by tannoy announcements that echo around the terminal like liturgies within cloisters.

He's vanished, gone, and done a Gran, Gail says.

Let's look downstairs, says red-tracksuit Jack. With that, now they were gone too.

Nathaniel has already ordered a coffee, and from his pine chair at the window, watches the anxious exchange between his children and lets them go. A slight breeze from the door cools his brow. His neatly combed hair is the colour of rock salt, a hint of dark at the crown. He is dressed in a blue cotton jacket, with two buttons on each sleeve, jeans, brown suede shoes with soles like soft summer beaches.

He takes a laptop from his leather satchel, and his winter-tanned right-hand closes around his mouth, suppressing a yawn. The tip of his thumb flicks his upper front teeth. Nathaniel takes a mouse from his bag and plugs it into the laptop. He beams a thin smile to the wood-panelled room to see if he has an audience and therefore exists. With his right hand, he massages the clean shaven, well moisturised folds of his neck and cheek, his blue eyes and face made ghostly by the glare from the screen. He sees someone looking at him, he smiles to make contact, but they look away. The tension in his neck eases.

The sound of a siren prompts others in the café to glance around and exchange nervous glances. Nathaniel doesn't look up from the screen. His left hand opens his blue shirt a little more so three buttons lie undone, and then he tugs at the frayed zip at the neck of his navy-blue jumper. He scratches the back of his head, and exhales a low tonal sigh, almost a word. He rests his chin against both his ringless hands, leaning on his elbows. He moves the screen with a finger, tongue brushing against the inside of his upper incisors and wetting his lower lip. His eyes turn sea green and lids flicker and close, the so-called laughter lines around his eyes appear worn thin like tissue paper and his eyes devoid of lustre or sparkle. He begins to type, looking at his fingers as he does so. He stops, and stabs impatiently at the space bar. He rubs his forehead with thumb and forefinger, then strokes a long earlobe. His hands fall flat on the table in front of him and clasp and unclasp in a sequence to an unheard rhythm. His lips move as he reads what he has written, he bites his right thumb and again runs his hand across an itch at the back of his head. Scrolling up and down the screen, he rereads again.

> *You give everyone what they want, and you use up all you have. You give someone everything you have, and it isn't enough. Sometimes you must say no and walk away.*

Fingers shield then close his eyes and his brows raise to reveal a stack of wrinkles. He picks at his nose. He sees someone watching him, a young mother with a noisy child, and looks away awkwardly.

His coffee arrives in a paper cup, he smiles at the young waitress, but she turns quickly and refuses to engage. He drinks with his right hand, and precisely places his left hand under his chin, covering his laptop and shirt from any drips that might show him up. His face darkens and he leans forward, arms crossed, to examine the words on the screen more closely. He notices the young mother staring at him again, looking at him whilst feeding her small child. He covers his face with the fingers of his right hand, and hits enter on the keyboard. His eyes water and rubbing his nose, his lips draw thin and old.

He stepped a few feet back as he watched Jack scatter the ashes, his hands shaking. When Jack threw the ashes from the pier head, face wet with tears, much of the anonymous looking dust went with the wind. Some of his mother landed in his eyes. Some in his hair. Even Nathaniel, standing back, tasted her ash, and some blew towards the ice cream shack and unknown to the young and so happily unaware vendor, ended up in the rum and raisin. They all laughed except the ice cream seller.

The compelling taste of salt in the air reminds him of how they were. Vapour trails in the darkening sky lead to places where he will be unknown. Contacts on his phone vanish, one after another.

The long summer evening light is gone, replaced by the cooling and damp and wrapping rags of sea mist that glow with diffused moonlight. He reaches the pier, and the boardwalk stretches out to an empty stage where Clare no longer stands. A tattoo of a lion drawn on her arm roars in his head, and the scent of rose twists into candy floss. The rest of the world is somehow getting on with it, yes, somehow, and he is no longer getting on with things. No one cares because no one knows. Or cares.

He passes the ice cream shack and hears an unseen audience

clapping from inside the theatre. The pier lights hang in a catenary chain, a ribbon that marks the way back to land. The clapping crowd is hidden, detached and absurd, animals hitting their paws together to signal endorsement of the pack. Sometimes these crowds are warm and loving as they were at the funeral, as despite being uninvolved in the busy administrative days before, he felt lifted by nearly a hundred hands, all of which had over a lifetime held her close, at some point had held her hand, and loved her almost as much and in some cases more than he thought he did.

But in the cold days after the funeral, after the wave of recognition, love and kindness recedes, death casually walks back into the room, taps him on the shoulder and reminds him that he remains disposable and alone.

A love letter in his pocket, the words of reconciliation he never sent, has become a sacred relic. Carrying it around, the paper sheets interrogate his soul and the envelope they are wrapped in, the envelope inscribed with her last address, rustles and reaches from his coat to hollow out his heart. Nathaniel throws the words into a litter bin and scrapes a safety match against sandpaper with a crack. A soft thrump and flare and the smell of sulphur is replaced by the bitter tongue of blackening ash. Reams of paper rustle then crump, releasing a blue-grey papal burst of smoke. Clank, clank and burning cardboard and chip paper flash to fire, and an empty coke can hisses as it rolls. The bin shudders and the flames leap high. He touches the rim of the bin and his fingers recoil with the sharp and angry heat.

Another round of hand clapping from the hall behind him. They sound very bored, the clap brief and impatient. He walks into the oat painted hall, yellow hued by weak and flickering wall mounted lights. Beside a side door to the auditorium, two elderly women smile at him kindly and offer warm white wine from white plastic cups. He looks through finger smeared windows, back to the dark shore, where the sea is metallic, cold, and utterly indifferent. Anger at loss doesn't travel well and dissipates as the incomprehension shallows, out there where others knew her less well.

Nathaniel looks out to see smoke drifting along the pier. Voices and words from the hall rise over seagull calls and grow to become shouts. A burning pier in the night creates a collective panic that runs quickly through the town. The flaming bin is quickly put out and this pier does not burn tonight. But in his head the pier burns into charred stumps in the sea, and he murmurs to himself—and whoever might be listening in a whisper Clare would have recognised—what is a seaside town without a pier?

Nathaniel walks to the shingle beach as the last of the smoke rolls down the flaking iron piles into the choppy incoming tide and becomes indistinguishable from the sea fog that is creeping from the south and west. He steps across the stench of rotting kelp forest collapsed and dried and full of flies. The edge of land, even when vile and decayed, feels safer than the unhappy sea veiled in mist. The wash, the rolling swish of shingle and the drawback, like a million fingers pulling knuckle deep through the small stones, drags the beach, and all the conversations of the day, back into the sea. The tide rakes them back for a moment, up to the land, then again with a slide of wet stones, flushes all back into the inky cold water. The partially dissolved words are thrown up, exposed one last time, and with a final flourish, the sea claws all back to the dark. He wanted no debate over wills, no arguments over what she didn't take with her. It wasn't his to take or even decide, so they could work it out themselves. No one likes disconnected relatives returning as tomb robbers. It doesn't matter, it is only junk and coin. They can't take her.

Death unlocks old love and decodes decisions. Over twenty years ago, they rejoined on this same pier, at the café which at that time still sold tea in polystyrene cups and flour-fingering mint imperials in paper bags.

Sit down, Nathan.

I am sitting down, Nathaniel said.

You are such a fidget fanny. American English, obviously.

Obviously.

Remember this, she said, throwing a photograph of them together down on the table.

Yes, he said.

Well, if we are to get back together, I need a few things agreed. Written in blood if necessary.

I agree, totally.

If I move, you need to cover all the bills until I find work.

Of course, I assumed that you'd need time to settle in.

And do you want kids?

Yes, yes, when the time is right.

No ifs or buts, do you want them or not?

Yes. Yes, I do. It will completely trash our lives but yes, I do.

What changed?

What?

You said you never wanted children.

So did you.

I am older now. And a little wiser. I think you might be too. If I'm going to pop a couple out, we are going to have to get on with it. And I've always enjoyed practicing making babies.

Yes, Clare, okay.

That doesn't sound enormously enthusiastic. I know what I'm talking about. Twenty plus years of sleepless nights, money worries and putting yourself second.

It's the putting myself second I worry about more.

You are not a completely selfish man, Nath.

Nope, he said, grabbing the last mint and placing it in her mouth.

You don't even like mint imperials, she said, vowels as wide and round and planetoid as the rocky sweet that rolled loudly around her mouth.

He left three years later. They had no children. Nathaniel sits and examines the photograph of them locked arm in arm on the beach. He places his thumb on her thumbprint. He imagines his hands resting on Clare's fingers, holding them one last time at the funeral directors. At twenty-two weeks, fingerprints are fully formed, Clare once said. They expand as you grow. He imagines a child's fingerprints added to the photograph. He thinks of the small fingers of an unborn child. He thinks of Clare's fingerprints, newly forged in her mother's womb when she herself was only twenty-two weeks old.

Grief forces time to align neatly backwards, so accident becomes predestination, story, and plot. Footsteps, those of the children he never had, the grandchildren he never could have had, and his first wife, all combine in the brine and disappear. Morning arrives with the tide and wipes the beach clean; today has become yesterday and the world a quieter place.

TILL DEATH DO US PART

Naili Huda

I asked about you like the woman in the story. You know, the woman who lost her son in the market. She went to the sugar merchant.

"Did you see a boy, of your chest height, a short while back? He's skinny and wearing a green striped t-shirt?"

"I might have seen him, but I am busy. I don't remember, sorry," the seller replied.

The mother who lost her child went to the next merchant. He owned a small flour shop.

"Did you see a boy walk past your shop recently?"

The elderly man shook his head.

The woman lost her son only a few hours ago, so she kept on looking. The market was big and crowded, but she did not lose hope.

She was busy buying bird-eye chillies from the local farmer when she lost the boy. They were holding hands at first, the mother and her only son, but then she needed to pick the freshest chillies. She always wanted the dark red, short ones, so she could get the right amount of burning hot sensation in her mouth upon eating them. The light red chillies would not have tasted so good.

When the woman selected the chillies, she let go of his hand unconsciously, and the boy moved aside to see the fresh tomatoes. There they were: red, yellow, orange, green—all shining. Then the boy went on to see the sweet potatoes: yellow, purple, small, big. Afterwards, he proceeded to the melons. Next the boy went on to the last stall. Then he disappeared. The next stall was the last in that row. You needed to turn left, right, or go straight if you wanted to explore the market more. The woman did not know which path the boy had taken. Driven by the mesmerising colours and shapes, the boy had forgotten his mother.

That's exactly how I asked about you too in the market.

"Did you happen to see Yogi near your place? He's black. The darkest one. You can barely see him at night."

"Have you seen Yogi? He's local."

"Have you seen Yogi? Every time he walks, his bottom swings to the left then right as his left back leg was once injured. Somebody brought him to me when he was a baby. He was found near a gutter, one leg strangled. Underweight, badly wounded, half limp, hungry and terrified."

"Did you happen to see Yogi? I named him that as his body was flexible, like a yoga teacher. He also had such wise eyes. You'd never forget him."

"Sorry."

"None to be seen."

The neighbours gave similar answers. It was maddening, you know. Losing something so dear to you. But the universe would not give a clue.

The woman in the market was lucky. She noticed her son was gone right away. Me? I had to wait until the next day to realise you did not come home that night. Your nocturnal habit reminded me to stay calm. But in the morning you were nowhere. Did a bat lure you with whatever fruit it got that night? Did you see a playful, mouth-watering mouse? Was it the sound of a night bird that you thought you might be able to catch?

Where were you? What did you do? How did you die? Where did you die? What killed you? I am aware that sometimes your kin choose to die away from their owners but I always hoped that wouldn't be you. Though it was you. How could you! It wouldn't have been a proper goodbye, I know, but at least you would not have left me with such killing curiosity.

You were sick. It was my fault. I always called off my plan to bring you to the vet. You saw I was busy with the office. Your swollen cheek got bigger and bigger, but otherwise, you looked okay. You were just as serene as your name, Yogi. Spoilt and confident. Coming to my lap whenever you wanted to. Or was that a sign for "Let's go to the vet now?" I intended to bring you once or twice but during those times you weren't home. Busy hanging out with the birds, aye? Darn, I am sorry. I should've tried harder. But what was it? Toothache? Virus?

It's funny we end up here like those pictures on the walls of medieval churches. What was the mistake you made, by the way? I am sinful. I deserve to be here. But you? To me you were always a cutie. You did more than ten friends could do together in easing my panic attack.

Once, I cheated on an exam but lied and said that I didn't. Now I feel as if my tongue has been pulled, cut, over and over again. The pain is enough to boil your brain. After this I will have another punishment for beating a man black and blue. That skinny bald man with a tattoo. He hit you in front of the house while you were trying to cross to the alley. It was a hit and run. I was so furious. A neighbour happened to recognise him and showed me his house. Anger held me so tightly, I attacked him like crazy without listening to his explanation.

Later I learned that his left eye was blind; he could not see you. He was in a hurry to get to his wife, who was in labour. He saw you were still alive, so continued his journey with the intention to return to check on you once his son was born safely. But it turned out that the premature child died in the womb. He then forgot to come to our house to apologise as he was mourning the death of his unborn son. I felt like the worst person alive after that, but what was done was done. The man's nose was fractured by my fist; his ugly face became uglier. There is no turning back.

Plastic surgery wasn't an option.

Uh oh, life. How hard it is to maintain positive thoughts.

Enough about my past mistakes. Now what did you do, beloved cat? Don't tell me you were suicidal from the bodily pain when you left home. You were? Woot. Then a car struck you when you were about to cross the road? Were you to meet your best friend?

Anyway. You died.

The new security man from the apartment at the corner just dumped you in the bin. How dare he! Sorry about that, Yogi. Pearls are pearls to a pearl seller, not to a blacksmith.

So you were mad at the way the security guard treated you? Then, with your supernatural powers you haunted him with whispers of guilt? Scared him as he had made a mistake? Dead cats should be properly wrapped and buried when they're dead. That's ancient wisdom. Pay respects to dead creatures. They're done with their life. It is time for them to continue the journey to the eternal. Nevertheless, he threw you like a piece of disgusting, dirty cloth. You saw it on his face when he lifted your body from the street? You were not a pretty sight at that time, though. You should've spared him. Did you really distract his mind when he was riding his motorbike? Did he swerve and die?

Yogi! You are so naughty.

You should have aimed to punish the car driver, not the security man.

You haven't forgotten about the car driver? Oh dear ... so that's why you've come back?

2.OUTSIDERS

AFTER A PARTY

Abigail Penny

No one called for you
    And made you twist your skirt hem
    No one ate the cake
And spat it in your face
No one gave you presents
That you had to smile at
The fireworks didn't go off
And make your ears explode
Your dog didn't bark
And piddle on the floor

The candles have burnt out
They would have done anyway
The pizza is cold
I don't like pepperoni
The party poppers lie intact
We can use them next time
That dress didn't get dirty
And neither did my hands
No one kissed your cheeks

The room is silent, the radio is off
You are in bed crying

THE ORPHANAGE

Costanza Casati

Italy, July 1973

"Do you miss our bedroom Julia?" Elisabetta whispered from her bed, her light blue eyes sparkling in the shadows. The other girls in the dormitory were already asleep: Julia could feel their regular breathing, like a lullaby cradling her. Too tired to reply, she pretended to sleep and joined the others in their rhythmic breathing. She felt her friend studying her in the dark, so remained still even though she wanted to move her legs into a more comfortable position. Eventually, she heard Elisabetta's light snoring.

Yes, she did miss their bedroom. Last year they had the privilege of sleeping in a semi-private room on the top floor of the orphanage's summer house. The two of them, unlike the other girls, were guests for a month's holiday as Elisabetta's mother was related to the abbess, Sister Amelia.

Julia didn't understand why her mother sent her: maybe she thought the beautiful countryside around Brescia was a good place for Julia to spend summer. The Sisters seldom let the girls out of the building anyways. But the year before, from the large window of their room, they had enjoyed the view of the countryside. Expanses of bright yellow rapeseed stretched to the horizon, interrupted only by dark brown fields covered in haystacks, that looked like careless brush strokes on canvas. The room had two small beds smelling of lavender and soap, and even a wardrobe where she and Elisabetta could stuff their belongings—not much though as unnecessary possessions like jewels or books were forbidden by Sister Amelia.

This year a new nun, Sister Grace, sturdy and tall with cold grey eyes, decided that Julia and Elisabetta should sleep in the main dormitory on the second floor which was chilly at night with high up windows. Julia could no longer enjoy the summer sunsets. In the mornings and evenings the light coming through the grey windows was all the same: shapeless, like the one cast through stained glass in church.

Julia stared at the ceiling, letting her mind wander around her big dreams and small hopes: she was a ballet dancer, no, an opera singer or a surgeon. She thought of a cone of whipped cream topped with cinnamon. Sister Amelia will never give me whipped cream, she considered, so she adjusted her thoughts and dreamt about fresh strawberries and melon instead. Wrapping her body in the blankets so that no part of her would be exposed to the air of the summer night, she willed herself to sleep.

Julia poured warm milk into her cup as she listened to Elisabetta's whispers about the latest orphanage gossip. Breakfast was in a big hall whose glass wall overlooked the internal courtyard, where a few bulky red birds were feeding. The eight long wooden tables were meant to bring the girls together. Still, most of them were eating their bread by themselves, shuffling their feet and sipping their milk as if lost in thought. Julia looked at Anna-Maria, an older girl staying in what was once Julia's bedroom. Everyone knew that two years earlier Anna-Maria had been adopted by a wealthy family from Milan, so no one understood why she returned to the orphanage's summer house. She had many clothes and even a portable radio that she listened to before going to bed without Sister Amelia complaining.

"Her new family don't want her during summer so they pay

for her to stay here," Elisabetta said.

"Why don't they want her?" Julia replied.

Anna-Maria, eating bread with jam, was sharing it with the girl next to her. Sara, a pretty blonde with a pale face and long legs was, like others in the orphanage, the daughter of a prostitute. Elisabetta was talking about *her* now.

"Sara's mother came here again last night with *that* man. Sister Amelia had a fight with him because they wouldn't leave."

"What does he want?"

Julia noticed a purple bruise on Sara's elbow.

"I've heard that he's her mother's *guardian* and he wants to be Sara's *guardian* as well." Elisabetta said the word with hesitation, unsure whether it meant something good or bad.

"That means the man wants Sara to be a prostitute," Julia said.

Elisabetta nodded. "But Sara doesn't want to. I heard that when they came last night she shouted at her mother, called her names then hid behind Sister Amelia."

Elisabetta's words died in her throat as Sister Grace walked behind her, checking if everyone had finished breakfast. The name Grace is the most inappropriate for her, Julia thought, there is nothing graceful about her: her steps on the floor are heavy, her fingers fat, her neck as thick as her head.

When the Sister was gone, Elisabetta moved closer to Julia on the bench.

"Sister Grace hits Lucia when she pees her bed at night."

Julia looked for Lucia. The girl was sitting by herself in a corner, her eyes downcast, her black hair falling around her head like a mudslide. The bread in Lucia's bowl was untouched. Julia finished her own bread and watched the sunlight coming through the windows, falling in golden shades on the floor and on Elisabetta's hair.

During the day they ate fresh strawberries in the yard and played hide and seek in the little church. When dinnertime came and the sky turned crimson, Julia noticed an excitement among the girls. They sat in the hall in little groups, whispered and ignored the carrot soup in front of them, from which a spiral of steam was rising. Elisabetta hurried to sit next to Julia, her braids swinging around her shoulders.

"The sisters!"

She pointed at two girls at the opposite end of their table. Julia recognised Clara and Angelica, the oldest at the orphanage. Clara was tall, with a muscular body and short straight hair that made her look like a boy. Angelica was slender, delicate, with a cascade of curly brown hair that covered her back completely. Everyone thought they hated each other since they barely talked and had nothing in common: Angelica always smelled lovely, like moisturising cream—Julia suspected she had hidden some under the mattress—while Clara didn't even shave her legs.

"What about them?" Julia asked.

The two seemed to be arguing: Clara slammed her fork on the table and grabbed her sister by the arm, shaking her whenever Sister Grace turned her back. Angelica shook her head in return, trying to escape from Clara's grip.

"Angelica wants to go out after bedtime to see the village boy she met!" No one ever left the orphanage to go to the nearby village of Chiari after dinner, not even the Sisters. Was Angelica mad? Julia remembered when, the week before, a young man with pastel green eyes had approached Angelica while the girls were on a trip to the old church.

"Sister Grace will find out," Julia said.

Elisabetta smiled.

"We'll see tonight."

Night came and no one could sleep. The girls turned in their beds, some sighed, others coughed. They heard Angelica's light footsteps as she left the room and the suffocated whispers of Clara who tried to hold her back. Afterwards, Clara walked to her bed and sat down under the blankets for a long time. Julia wondered if she was praying. She tried to picture Angelica's small figure walking on the country road under the stars to meet the man of her life. A forbidden love. How brave, how beautiful she was.

A shout. Blows, one after the other, followed by moans. The heavy steps of Sister Grace on the stairs that went up to the dormitory from the dining hall. The lights were on. In between the rows of beds, Sister Grace was dragging Angelica towards the toilets. The girl was wearing her best white summer dress, the one she wore to Sunday mass. The girls watched in silence while Sister Grace pulled Angelica's hair as if it were a horse's mane. Only Clara got up from her bed, her pyjamas too large for her lean figure, making her look like a ghost.

"Stop it," she said.

The nun ignored her and entered the bathroom. Julia and Elisabetta followed. Angelica hid her face behind her hands, wet with tears.

"Aren't you ashamed? We've given you a home!" Sister Grace said.

Clara seemed frozen, her arms hanging down the sides of her body, her face as white as Angelica's dress. Sister Grace drew the curtain of a shower, turned on the freezing water and dragged Angelica under it. Angelica hit her head and started screaming, her dress shrank, sticking to her arms and chest as if sewn onto her skin. Julia couldn't breathe. More girls were watching now. The scene was performed by Sister Grace as a warning, a lesson.

Clara stepped forward. She grabbed the metallic bin from under the sink and hit the Sister's back with it. Stained tampons and tissues spread on the wet floor.

Clara pushed Sister Grace away, positioned herself in front of her sister and turned the shower off. A strand of hair fell out of Sister Grace's veil and made her look lost for a second.

Then: "Go to bed," Sister Grace said.

Julia ran and hid under the blankets, her heart beating fast. She heard Sister Grace walking away, then lighter steps and a soft weeping. When she peeked out of her nest, Clara and Angelica sat on a bed, hugging and trying to warm each other.

BORDERING

Elif Gulez

The coffee van, red and shiny, stood in between the neighbours' Tesla and Jag. Ferya and Hasan were business owners now; the van was their ticket to permanent residency. Hasan, formerly a white-collar employee, now woke up at five to work fourteen hours a day, in a cold and rainy climate his body refused to adjust to, without a roof above his head. When his round was over, the couple tidied up the van with high hopes and naïve determination: they were going to change their luck.

Soon after the van's arrival, one of the neighbours, an old lady with grandmotherly looks, stopped Hasan on the pavement and said: "You know, you can't park a commercial vehicle here. There's a clause saying so in the title deed."

Hasan said he didn't know.

"Do you see any other vans around?" asked the nice lady.

She added: "I'll give you a chance to move it out, and if you don't, I *will* make an official complaint."

Later on, the owner of the Jag repeated the same thing.

"A rule is a rule," said Hasan.

He parked the car in a parking space outside the lodge. A week passed and a man called out from across the street: "You know, ever since you've started parking this van on the street, crossing the road has become extremely dangerous for pedestrians. The height of the van is blocking our vision."

Hasan opened his mouth as if to say: *The van isn't taller than the SUVs parked on both sides of the road,* but he didn't say anything. Instead, he moved the van to a spot further down the road.

But citizens raised their concerns about the van one after another, the next day, and the next, and the next. And with each complaint, Hasan moved the van a little further. And he kept on going, until one day the van was nowhere to be seen.

RESTAURANT OF THE HEART

Elise Heath

The building nestles in the middle of a residential estate, behind a primary school. Whenever I go, the parents are walking their children home for lunch. When they look at me, their grip on that little winter coat gets tighter, and they pull the child aside to let me speed past on my long legs. As I get closer to my destination, the small houses turn into high rise tower blocks, all the same dull grey-yellow, like faded Lego bricks.

Once a shocking sight to me, the epitome of poverty, these ugly buildings, often with piles of junk or laundry hanging on their tiny balconies, have become a part of my everyday life, although I've yet to step a foot inside one.

I walk through car parks, across cracked concrete and patches of mud where grass once was. I turn the corner, and there it is, the doorway. Sometimes the van is parked outside, with *Les Restaurants du Cœur* painted on the side in bold black letters over a bright pink heart between a knife and fork. Otherwise there is no indication of what's through the door. An A4 sheet handwritten notice reminds visitors to report to reception. It might be ominous, if it weren't written in coloured highlighter pen.

Once inside, I feel tension slip out of my body, as I unwind my scarf from around my neck and head for the office, smiling and saying *Bonjour* to every familiar face. I dump my layers of winter wear on the coat rack and pin my name tag to my chest, with its little heart and knife and fork. A badge of honour, a shield of status. It says: *I know what I'm doing,* even if I don't.

After the obligatory *Ça va* tennis with other volunteers (everyone *is* well, of course), I pick up a clipboard with a pen attached by green string. Jean Luc adds another green sheet to the pile, so I take it and clip it to my board.

As usual, I hope the name atop the sheet will give away who I am looking for but, as usual, I have no preconceptions attached to non-English names. I pronounce it as best I can, but it's not until my third try that a woman steps forward. She is shorter than me, which is rare, and she has brought her son with her.

"Call me Louise," she says.

I introduce myself, and she introduces her son.

"He's come to help me."

We shake hands.

"Only one person going round," a voice interrupts.

It's Anne-Marie, leaning in as she walks past with her client.

"Children can wait in that room; there's cake."

I feel the hairs on the back of my neck stand up. Although she spoke to Louise, she looked at me, and I get the feeling I'm being evaluated. Louise reluctantly sends her son off to the waiting room, and Anne-Marie leads her client to the dessert section but I imagine her crossing off on her clipboard, marking me down.

Trying to remain positive, I ask Louise if she's been here before (she has) and make small talk while we queue at the meat counter. I always struggle to find topics to talk about. What if I ask what job they do and they're unemployed? What if I comment on the cold weather and they're actually homeless?

"How old is your son?" I ask.

I'm pleased because children are always a safe topic, for people who have them.

"Eleven," she replies.

"So he's just started secondary school?"

"No, next year."

I cringe. I still haven't got to grips with what ages are in which year groups, even though I've been teaching in schools for months. Louise has noticed the woman in front of us, who is wearing a black hijab and has two little children in tow. They make eye contact and Louise asks, "These your kids?"

The woman smiles, obviously proud.

"They made my son wait in there," Louise gripes.

I feel that bristling on the back of my neck again.

"Sorry," I say. "It gets quite crowded."

When we arrive at the front of the meat counter I say hi to the man and woman who work there then zone out while they go through Louise's options with her.

When we get to the dairy section, I grab the two cartons of milk that Louise, as a two-person household, is entitled to, and ask her which yoghurts she wants. I put a pack of *Natur* in her big shopping bag and wait for her to pick more.

"More?" she asks, unable to believe it.

She's not the only one.

"You have nine points for yoghurts, and those yoghurts are four for one point."

Louise looks indecisively at the range of yoghurts, none of which have fruity or chocolate flavours. They all look the same to me but that's because I'm lactose intolerant. And English. She reaches into the fridge to look.

"Please don't touch the items, Madame," comes that voice again.

Anne-Marie is by my side, practically snatching yoghurts from Louise's hands. She snaps at me. "It's *you* who picks up the items."

As if I have forgotten my great honour.

The back of my neck bristles.

We get through the vegetable section without incident. Louise doesn't really like to cook, preferring cartons of pre-made soup and bags of dried pasta. She doesn't use up all her points. I scold myself for judging her rejection of fresh vegetables. Not everyone has the time or energy to cook. Maybe she doesn't have a big kitchen.

At the pastries, she asks to see this and that, and I pick up the packets from the top shelf, offering them to Louise, before putting them back when she decides it's not for her. Anne-Marie snaps at Louise: she's indecisiveness, she's manhandling the croissants, she's holding everyone up. Louise can see I'm flustered. She says she'll take another pack of kiddie brioche and we move on to the desserts.

We take some fruit, but Louise rejects all the sugary things. Still she has points left. The clementines have nil points because there are so many to get rid of. I give Louise more and more. Kiwis are one point each, so again I give her more and more.

Then, Anne-Marie swoops in. Louise has taken too much, she accuses. I try to explain that I have been counting but I feel like my French fails.

I came here to meet local people, to get involved in the community. But the community is divided. The people don't trust me to follow their rules. The volunteers, all white French pensioners, have never left their corner of France. They don't trust newcomers. I have noticed their quiet suspicion of the women in hijab, but now realise the extent of this hierarchy between who is a volunteer and who is a client.

"You have to be aware that some people take advantage."

I swallow my thoughts. They take advantage of the charity that is specifically designed to help them? They take the food that they are offered? Even if it had exceeded her "points", were a few kiwis worth this fuss? How could you reduce a person to "points" they are allowed to have?

I am just "la jeune anglaise" or "Brexit". The volunteers other me with nicknames. I cannot understand, they tell me. *Your* country, England, is in disarray, they tell me. We won't let ours fall apart too, they say. They make sure to pay me to take the bus to their big houses, to tutor their own children English. But if a woman on benefits takes too many kiwis, who knows what could happen?

3. WE CAN BE HEROES

LIFE LESSONS FROM LOBSTERS

Ankit Agrawal

There's an interesting urban myth about lobsters.

When you cook a pot of male lobsters, you have to keep a lid on the cooking pot because when males realise they're in a pot of boiling water, they try to escape even though they know it is futile. On the contrary, when cooking female lobsters, you don't need to put a lid on the pot. Female lobsters know there's no point fighting a fight which is already lost. Female lobsters hold their claws and brace each other for the impending doom.

This theory, casting males as heroic but stupid and females as practical and supportive, is, of course, factually incorrect. All lobsters have a ganglionic nervous system. They do not feel pain. Boiling or steaming them is the most humane and quickest way to kill a lobster you want to eat, assuming you are not a vegetarian.

However, a question about life has been illustrated. Should we die fighting or surrender to the whims of time?

Knowing when to quit is equally important as knowing how to keep on fighting. Of course, perseverance and never backing down from a challenge are desired qualities, if you want to be successful in life, relationship or career. There are a thousand reasons for continuing with something past the point where you should stop.

However, more often than not we consider striving for gold as the only norm for success because giving up is labelled cowardly. Many of the "buts" are mostly a figment of the imagination, a case of mistaken identity. You and your goals are two separate things.

We sugar-coat the rationale for not backing off with the psychological name of atychiphobia, fear of the unknown or the self-inflicted need of not causing a social uproar by upsetting others because we falsely assign safety and entropy to perseverance and persistence. This obsession with never giving up is not perseverance, it is blind persistence. Blind persistence eventually turns any quest into an exhausting and useless ordeal.

It is logical to think that if we were to endure a little longer then maybe with time we will fix the problems and reach our goals. However, sometimes our very attempts to fix things might be having a negative impact on them as well as on us. So, is it not sometimes imperative to give up, just plain, and simple, to STOP.

If we let go of our goals and other trivial quests can't they readily be replaced with other and better goals? But what about jobs, relationships, and friendships? After all, they are not easy to come by, one must work for them. To that I say only this. Sure, working toward a worthwhile goal is elating but the moment you lose excitement about your achievements you understand that it is not what you wanted, it is not catering to your innate desires. As Cloris Kylie says: "You've become used to striving and never arriving."

But how to determine if it's time to give up? The simplest solution is asking this question of yourself. What would my life be if I just stopped trying to solve everything? If your inner aura answers "freedom and exhilaration", then it's time you gave up on it.

I spent half a decade working for a company I didn't want to work for. I even rejected a job I actually wanted to do because I had fallen into the agenda of the city I was in. The advice I needed to hear was: "What the hell are you doing? Give this up." Not that it wasn't offered, but I didn't listen.

In the end, I did quit and it was hard. At first, it was horrible. Amongst my friends there were a fair few failure-phobes and those who preferred the dull path. Few respected that knowing when to say no is the bravest decision. Most admired trying and failing. But I fed the inner best, my biggest asset—myself.

I did suffer temporary pain, emotional trauma or remorse, but once I overcame these negative emotions, I welcomed loving and uplifting thoughts into my life, opening a door to fulfilling and joyful life experiences, setting me on a path of learning, growth, and expansion!

According to Monica Geller:

1. Just Listen to yourself
2. Re-tally your numbers
3. Get outside evaluation
4. Be ready to rip off the plaster
5. Take atychiphobia head on
6. Vanquish the "what if" worm, and
7. Remember the cost of opportunity.

Sometimes the real heroes are those who know when best to retreat.

I AM KATHERINE MARGARET HALL, THE WONDER WOMAN

Katie Margaret Hall

Shortlisted for the Word Poetry Competition 2019

The Wonder Woman
   who was unexpected. A perfect coincidence of nature and
     time.
Who has battle scars as badges
of past victories and defeats. Who carries a shield
instead of a sword
to defend her honour. Who has a cape
and fights for those who cannot,
with her heart and soul and action. Who stands
in the shadows of giants, owning her place
at their side. Who loves no matter what

and no matter how worn through.

Who is named for the warriors who came before
and passed down the mantle.
I am wonder woman.
I am Katherine Margaret Hall.

FALSE GOD

Cheryl Powell

Published in Flash Fiction Magazine 2019

When she stepped off the motorway bridge at Long Hampton, she was well prepared to meet God. She'd rehearsed for months. It mattered that she remembered to tell him everything: how he was scum, how she hated him, how she would tear his sanctimonious head off, side with the Devil against him. It was important she left nothing out.

Split seconds before she pitched off the windscreen of a Mitsubishi four-by-four, she let God have it. She cursed his egotistical and spiteful ways, and railed against his lack of pity. She upbraided him for his fakery, his spurious show of love and compassion. His chance to save the child. Yes, in the gathering velocity, her fists breaking the fall, she remembered the whole diatribe, and spat it in his face.

What she didn't remember was this: a tiny hand in hers, a first tooth put by for the fairies, ridiculous bath-times in a wonky sink. She didn't remember those huge eyes lost in delight at a bedtime story, or a pink worm wriggling. Nor did she remember joy, or wonder, or that breath-stopping stab of unconditional love.

As it happened, God took it well. It was nothing he hadn't heard before. He shrugged and smiled and picked up all those unremembered moments, counting and sifting them; he knew every single one by heart. Then he locked them away in his secret drawer. And waited. One day, he knew, she would come to him, on her knees, and beg him for the key.

4.VILLAINS

GRAVEYARD GUARDIAN

Cameron Yanoscik

My voice; the only sound in the soundless night. Night, hiding my presence, is felt by those who know I am theirs. Theirs. I watch over, float over, forever. Forever will I spend, lying awake, among those in eternity's rest.

I stalk a churchyard, "haunting ground" if you will, as I have done before and will do again. In dog shape, mist form, I come. As a floating, light, gargoyle-winged creature, I lurk. Or in visage of the human mortal I once possessed from eons ago.

It is difficult to piece together the circumstances that led me to my fate. That of: caretaker of ghosts, keeper of souls, protector of shades.

I am a *Graveyard Guardian*.

I do not love the profession that was forced upon me so violently. I have just merely accepted it, come to terms with it, throughout time, as time I now possess. Those who ruthlessly shed my body from my soul, flung my corpse into an earthen mound which they first dug up, then covered over and left not to rot, but to take on new life. My transition to the hereafter, the netherworld, Hades, *HeavenandHell,* was for their selfish purposes. It did not matter that they buried me alive, I was only to serve their purpose, not mine.

Did I have a destiny, a fate to begin with? Or was I forever marked? To be cooped up in the boneyard, moulded in the graveyard and fenced in within the cemetery? To be: watcher of graves, viewer of tombstones, crosses and crypts.

I am the *Graveyard Guardian*.

I have seen the living and the dead, all, in dead communion with each other. Tears have been shed, wails have been heard, the dirt has been dug up, set in and coffins lowered into sunken beds, made to last for all time. Stones crack, are washed away, eaten away, wiped away. And yet the souls remain while their bedclothes are in disarray.

And yet ... I remain. And always will.

In the sounds of the soundless night, my presence is known. The living, passing by on absent-minded journeys, on evenings, have dared to come close and have tasted my wrath. I howl, I bark, I scream. Floating amongst the grey pillars and stones, I am a thing of dread, a thing of fear. Then they see me there. And run.

I am the commander of the unseen. God did not will it, only Man. Man created me. Made me: spectre of the sepulchral and phantom among phantoms. Of ghosts and spirits. Of my restful dead. For all are at rest here, except for me. I am keeper of shades, protector of souls, caretaker to this immense necropolis, which I will haunt forever more. No rest have I, I who am awake among the dead.

Only Doomsday provides hope. Judgement Day may bring some redeeming light. Will God reward me for my work? Will I transcend, on wings of glory, to Paradise to be with my kin? Will I be among those who watched silently as my soon-to-be-lifeless form was made cornerstone to this city of the dead, on the outskirts of a humble village, those centuries ago?

In dog form, as phantom ghost and mist, dost I descend. I haunt, I lurk, I stalk, I watch and I wait. I leer, I scowl, I bare my teeth, rattle chains, fly, hover, spook, shift and disappear. And as always ... I wait.

My warnings break the silence of the night. My breath provides charms to the charmless. I am theirs. I look after, watch over, huddle them to my breast as infant children to a once nurturing mother.

I am. I was. I will be: "good caretaker", spirit protector and souls' keeper.

They call me Church Grim or *Kyrkogrim*. And so, I am their *Graveyard Guardian*.

I am the *Graveyard Guardian*. I am, and will simply be, the *Graveyard Guardian*.

So, beware.

WHAT WE SEE

Miloni Shah

"Kala, kali, kala kaloota, kali kalooti, kala kauwa, kali kauwi."

This is what dark skinned people grow up listening to in homes, in schools, in playgrounds, in workplaces.

Research by Swedish economists in 2013 shows that India is the least racially tolerant country in the world. 43.5% of Indians don't want neighbours from a different race. This is despite the fact that India was one of the first countries that recognised colonial abuse and fought for its freedom. We set an example for the world. We knew what it felt like when someone discriminated against us on the basis of our colour and race. We've been victims for two hundred years. We've risen. We know what it took to fight such discrimination.

Yet, we are the least racially tolerant country in the world. We don't question movies and songs with racist content. In fact, we watch them. Multiple times. We dance to songs that directly or indirectly look down upon a section of race.

[*Fashion* by Madhur Bhandarkar] "Priyanka Chopra sleeps with a black man."

There's only one interpretation to it: Your career and your life are at an all-time low. You have fallen to the lowest of the low. Time to get your shit together.

India is a conservative country. As a society, sex and talking about sex is a taboo. More so if it is done before marriage. We bypass all our conservative thoughts when a woman sleeps with a black man. Meanings change with the colour of a person's skin and our eyes on it.

Africans who come to India suffer racial prejudice. You read the news reports. Name-calling. Staring. Gawking. In shops, in restaurants, in slums, walking down the streets, their neighbourhood or their society. Men thrashed. Women abused - verbally, physically and sexually. Assaults and attacks don't stop when the Indian government releases guidelines and advertisements to protect Africans.

Black skin cannot be unseen.

> *African students assaulted. 29-year-old Congolese woman killed. Mob attacks a Tanzanian woman—beaten and stripped naked. African men beaten inside a security booth—bare hands, sticks and shoes.*

Be it Delhi, Mumbai or Bangalore.

Racism is real.

Superheroes and villains. Indian television serials and Bollywood films. White equals purity. Most heroic Indian actors who are successful have a light skin tone. Few Indian actors who are brown, Akshay Kumar and Ajay Devgan, have been a little more successful. Actors like Johnny Lever, Rajpal Yadav and Prakash Raj are either assigned comic or villainous roles. Brilliant actors. Loved by everyone. But never the heroes. Never the winners. When fair-skinned celebrities play the role of the villain, a certain amount of make-up is applied to make their tone darker. Few brown Indian actresses have been successful. But *their* skin tone borders on dusky and not a shade darker, for example Deepika Padukone and Bipasha Basu. For the other heroines, Katrina Kaif, Jacqueline Fernandez, Aishwarya Rai, Alia Bhatt; it's not important if they don't act well - they just need to look pretty and fair.

The same applies to Indian television serials. Mostly watched by the older generation—the stay-at-home wives and the stay-at-home husbands. Female roles will be played by a fair-skinned actress. Only the servants or the villains will have a darker skin tone. Komolika in a negative role in *Kasauti Zindagi Kay*. Brown. Rajja, the servant, in *Baa Bahoo aur Baby*. Brown. Tulsi, the perfect bahu, in *Kyunki Saas Bhi Kabhi Bahu Thi*. Fair.

Abhay Deol wrote about this racism and his experiences in the *Hindustan Times*. His mindset changed only when he went abroad. When suddenly he became a person of colour.

The fairness creams in India are a million-dollar industry, he says.

The actors propagating it shouldn't be blamed. It is for the people of India to change their mindset first.

Newspapers should be more vigilant of the advertisements that they accept, he says.

At the same time, we applaud when one of our own makes it on Western shores. How can we ask those in the West to be aware of their racism when we are unaware of our own? And how are we connected to Asia in this mass obsession for "white" skin? Stop asking actors why they continue to endorse such brands, because you continue to advertise them! Don't ask advertising executives why a brand uses language and imagery in this country that they would apologise for in other countries. They do this because *you* continue to look for a "fair" bride or bridegroom in your matrimonial ads, and because *you* continue to point the finger away from yourself.

Fair. Slim. Beautiful.

The first line of each matrimonial page. We, as a society, have a colonial hangover. We believe in white supremacy. Traditionally, we've never given colour a thought. Never analysed and segregated humans. Colonisation has ingrained several concepts into our minds, hearts and souls: The fairer you are, the prettier. More attractive. More educated. More touchable. Face wash, cream, powder.

Pond's White Beauty Anti Spot Fairness Day Cream, Pond's White Beauty Spotless Lightening Face Wash, Fair and Lovely Winter Fairness Face Cream, Fair and Lovely Fairness Face Wash.
Mix: Besan, curd, honey and lemon. Apply layers and layers on your skin.

The cold, smelly, gooey liquid. On your face, your neck, your hands, your legs. Every visible layer of your skin. Let it dry. Rub it. The dried powder will prick your skin. Scrub it. Let it hurt you. Get rid of the tan. Make your skin lighter. Get rid of the evidence that you went swimming. To the beach. Played catch or hide and seek with your friends for a few hours. We don't want that colour. Apply the sticky stuff one coat after another. Don't forget to scrub a lemon peel. Of course the transparent drops will sting your skin. Worth it. Because only then will someone like you. Only then will someone love you. Only then will someone marry you.

According to Forbes, in 2014 Bollywood produced 1602 films. Bollywood earned a gross box office of 1.59 billion dollars. Shahrukh Khan alone earned 600 million dollars. The general public admires Bollywood actors. Will go through a snowstorm if need be to shake their hands. Even if their films are a flop, these actors will still earn huge profits. People watch films for the actors in it. The fair and handsome. Shahrukh Khan endorsed this brand. Now Siddharth Malhotra. White skin is the norm.

White is not a colour. Anything other than white is a colour. The rest of us are "persons of colour".

Atithi devo bhava, which means, "The guest is equivalent to God" or "Be one for whom the guest is God". It is a Sanskrit verse, taken from an ancient Hindu scripture which became part of the "code of conduct" for Hindu society. Our basic principle. About time we put it to use.

MISPLACED

Patrick Cronin-Coltsmann

The woman sat up upon the grey dirty ground beneath her and blinked.

She scrunched her eyes and tried her best to peer through the smothering fog, she could only make out the stretch of ground about her. Barren and grey in every direction.

There had been a car, it was driving the wrong direction.

She shouted, but her voice was swallowed up in the thick bowels of the omnipresent fog.

Her shouting turned to pleading and tears swelled in her eyes. She clenched dirt in her fists, it crumbled to dust and slipped between her fingers.

Eventually, she picked herself up off the floor.

She held herself in her arms and strode into the fog. She noticed no change in it or the ground underfoot.

The woman kept striding. It was interspersed with further calls, always left unanswered. Her stride turned to an amble, and then, to a shuffle. Then she stopped, crouched down and gathered herself, before setting off once more.

This process repeated for some time. She neither hungered nor thirsted. Nor tired. She could not sleep when she lay herself down.

Eventually, she stopped calling.

She tried to draw upon the ground, in that lifeless dirt. But she found that no matter how long she had spent carving groove after groove, as soon as she shifted her gaze, the ground beneath was featureless once more. She tried to dig, but beneath the stale topsoil was stone she could not so much as mark.

And so she passed time in her imagination, pretending she was not in that colourless, empty place. But with time the effort grew too much, and she lost her spark.

She tried to talk to herself, her only company. Her conversations started quaint and quirky, her sole injection of cheer, however forced and however false. They soon became terser. It did not take long before she stopped altogether and nary a whisper escaped her tight lips.

Thus she wandered in that endless fog, for days. And the days turned to months. And the months to years.

The dirt had no taste, and nor the fog, and nor did she. She had long since given up on harming herself, she could pound upon the under-stone for hours, and she did, without a scratch upon her knuckle nor tinge of pain. She could breathe fistfuls of dust and not need to cough.

And the years turned to decades.

She had stopped walking. Her prison was boundless. She lay curled upon the drab ground and what semblance of her sanity she retained she kept by counting, higher and higher. Higher than she ever could have imagined she would be able.

And the decades turned to centuries.

Eventually, she stopped thinking.

And the centuries turned to millennia.

And the millennia turned to aeons.

SOAP

Thea Etnum

"Wicked woman," he muttered.

His words irked me. I never really see myself as a woman, I thought.

"I never really see myself as a woman," I told him.

"Do you mind if others do?" he asked. "Besides, you're not just wicked; you're also—fun."

"Of course, wicked and fun—I'm a cliché."

"Exactly," he smiled.

"Get off me, and get out."

I put my cold feet on Ramkumar's chest and pushed his naked body away. It was so hairy, it felt warm. There were two sides to naked men, like to anything else out there. The good warm side felt almost like nestling inside thick grass—or hay, but a smooth kind of hay—and awfully sexy. But with a hairy man, there is less skin to touch, less contact; there is always a layer in-between.

I stared at Ram's dark body as he got out of bed and started fidgeting about. I felt I wanted to stick my fingers into all that hair again.

"I want to stick my fingers into your back hair—and take it out by the roots. You really should shave it, I keep telling you. Or I could do it—more *wicked* fun for me."

"Whatever. I need to shower and go to work ... I have a job, unlike some people."

"What's that supposed to mean? I'm a student," I said, and put both my hands behind my back in mock compliance. I was completely naked, watching him fumbling around in the same state. Adam and Eve, post-sin; post-Eden, in the crammed limbo of my small student residence room. This particular Adam cursed as he tripped on something and almost fell through the bathroom doorway. I knew it wouldn't be long until he would be back out again.

"What now?" I asked, bored.

"This," he answered and stretched out his hand. Lying flat on his palm was my tiny bar of soap, worn into a wafer-thin oval, about the size of a child's ear. "Is this all you've got?" He seemed scandalised.

"Oh no you don't," I cried. "Not with all the hair on that body of yours! You're not using *my* soap."

"What's left of it," he said with a puzzled look. "I'll buy you more next time. Didn't know things have been so bad for you."

"Hey, that's expensive stuff, I'll have you know."

"Fine, I'll buy you some expensive soap, then."

"No, don't buy me soap. Just don't."

"Why not?"

"Because—it would only remind me of unpleasant stuff. Childhood stuff."

I tried to keep cool as I got up, pulled his oversized fluorescent gym shirt on, and got ready for some soul-baring. I knew he was still watching me.

"So, I sang carols with a choir one winter, Christmas-time, when I was about six. It was for the German embassy. After we'd sung, they gave us these carefully wrapped bars of soap as Christmas presents."

"That's all?"

"No, there's more to it than that—"

"No, I mean, is that all you got from the embassy people?"

"No, we also got parcels of winter tea, and that made sense as a Christmas gift. But the soap … that was just …"

"What? The soap was just what? Other than given to you as a present for having sung an off-key version of an obscure Christmas carol?"

Ramkumar's eyes were half-closed, his mouth dancing to the side in the suggestion of a crooked smile. He was secretly congratulating himself on his last question, I could tell.

"We were not off-key at all. We sang *Stille Nacht*. German carols —German Embassy. And you'd better shut up and listen, because I've just begun telling you my sad story."

"Could it get any sadder than this?" He puffed and held the fragile piece of soap between his fingers.

"How many times do I have to tell you? That is an expensive soap. Careful with it."

"So you keep saying. It looks very expensive indeed." He stared at it as if that would make it enlarge. "And what the hell happened to your light?" he asked. He pulled the bathroom chord only to hear a click-click that ignited nothing.

"Just leave the door open, Ram, and you'll have enough light."

"Alright, Dirty One. I'll do that," his words echoed from inside the bathroom.

"Hey, I'm not dirty. I do wash."

"Whatever, Dirty."

It was as if he was inside a cave. That's how his words sounded. A caveman in the bathroom cave, all sweaty and weary. Getting ready for office work. But the hunting season had been long gone for this caveman, and that ignited frustration. The only thing he would be hunting for now was the wicked species; like myself.

I started to turn the lights of my room on and off, flicking the switch over and over. "Come out and join the disco, Mighty Samson," I yelled. "Leave washing for another time. And do the same with your job. You're rich, who cares?"

His face emerged once again. His eyes were dark and wide and I wondered if there was anything more to be discovered within them. Any other expression that they were capable of, something that I hadn't already seen? And I had seen quite a lot of him.

"No shampoo," I confessed, beaming.

It was just such fun to see his rich boy's face contorting with confusion and anger, all at once. Good thing he'd washed at the gym the night before, otherwise who knew what might not have happened between us.

"Stop playing with the lights!"

"I won't stop. Not until you listen to the rest of my story."

"What story?" He was exasperated. "I have to go to work and I can't even wash. I don't have time for stories."

"My soap story—"

"Whatever. I'm going to wash with plain water. I'll just put on my spare clothes."

I heard something like a snort when he went inside the cave and closed the door. His t-shirt still had a faint smell of sweat, carefully disguised by expensive after-shaves and lotions. I inhaled. There were a lot more notes in that smell than I had ever seen in his eyes.

He came out of the bathroom again in no time, sullen, water dripping all over.

"What?"

"A towel?"

He seemed so fragile, standing naked in the door of the bathroom, his eyes wandering around the room, trying to figure out where he'd put his clothes. So vulnerable. A towel, I thought, at least I could give him that.

"Hey, have you seen my bag anywhere?" he asked, dripping himself dry.

His clothes were in his black gym bag, the one I'd pushed under the bed. I'd tripped on it the previous evening while he'd been brushing his teeth. I'd started zipping and unzipping it until it broke. It had stuck open with the zip-teeth all out of synch, so I had pushed it under the bed and didn't say a word. He could search for it while I finished my story.

"I don't know about your bag. It has to be here somewhere, just look around. So, where was I?"

"Dancing. You were dancing for the German Embassy."

"Dancing? No, I was singing."

"Yeah, that's what I meant. Where's my stuff?"

He was bending, half-naked—how did the ancient Greeks find beauty mainly in the male body, I thought. I saw no grace or beauty in that. It meant other things to me.

"No idea…"

I sat down on the bed, my legs deliberately obscuring the part where I'd kicked his bag.

He was fumbling around, still dripping. Like a dark ice sculpture, melting; the towel wasn't helping him much.

"So, what happened? Tell me the story already. Jeez, my bag is under your bed. Move your legs!"

I looked out of the window as he shoved my legs to the side. He was struggling to reach his bag while I was struggling to finish my story.

"I was with my little sister Rosa in the carol choir, on that Christmas Eve. She was a lovely little girl back then. Nice and sweet, didn't speak much. Anyway, she had this condition. An eating disorder. We didn't understand it then. She would basically eat stuff that was not quite food: dirt, glue, paper. And that night, it was the soap. She'd begun nibbling on the bar she'd been given, when Mama saw her…"

I kept looking out of the window as I was telling the story. I could hear Ram's movements slow down.

"The choir mistress had also seen her doing it and she told my mother to get Rosa checked, because there was probably something terribly wrong with my sister. Especially since, when they tried to take the soap away from her, she got almost aggressive." I hugged my knees to my chest and pulled my t-shirt further down as I was talking, taking it from my ankles to my toes, covering myself.

"But Mama was the aggressive one. When she saw Rosa with the soap, she started hitting her. I couldn't do anything. I was terrified of my mother and her bouts of fury. Mama made my sister walk around for a whole month with plasters on her mouth, or stay with her hands tied behind her back so that she would be forced to give up her habit. It was simply awful. But Mama was an awful person. And I think it was that very moment—the exact moment, yes—when I stopped believing in the idea of family. Eight years old, I was."

Only then did I turn to Ram, scrutinising him; his eyes were round with amazement. No visible emotion though, just surprise.

"Wow. Interesting story. But I'll need my t-shirt back," he said, reminding me that I was wearing something that did not belong to me. "So, what happened with your sister?"

"She's fine now, as far as I know." That's all I said, as I took the t-shirt off and was naked once again.

When Ram left, he mumbled something about how I should take care, and do some shopping; and that I should probably phone my sister.

"I don't have a sister."

The words came out of my mouth after he'd gone out of my room and the door slammed behind me with a bang. Those insufferable doors.

I picked the small soap up, then prudently took just a tiny bite of it. It didn't taste like I'd remembered it from childhood, back in the days when my mom called me by my other name, Rosa. I'd never had a sister.

Ram had put his money next to the soap, on my desk. He left me more. He always left me more money for one night than I'd ever asked for, to help with tuition and whatnot. Plus, we'd got close. He was one of the likeable clients. I had only a few, and fewer still were likeable. Even though Ram was practically married, which of course took some points out of his overall likeability score.

But once again, much like his personality, that was simply not my problem.

5.GIRLHOOD

ON READING MISS BRILL

Abigail Penny

I hope I'm lucky to live long enough
to own a fox pelt
I hope I'm lucky enough
to watch my hands become tree roots
and have young boys mock me
in front of their girls
I hope I live long enough to disgust them
with my very presence
and cry every evening I'm alone
with a cake slice to bear me through it.
But the future is a far
and long enough place
It's a bargain I haven't made yet
there's still time for song
and people to watch
I've yet to buy my fur

But with every strand of silver I find
or every new wrinkle near my eye
I see the future is very near and very short

the length between your maiden name
and your title
it's a bargain I'm not sure I want to make
for all the bands that play
and all the people to watch
none of them will be playing
or watching out for me

50-EAST

M Rene Bradshaw

A barrage of splintering Spanish leaked over Officer Sachamo Soto's cubicle and into the waiting area inside the portable trailer. In the midst of the pandemonium engulfing the cottages that day, Florentina sought out the Spanish, the language of her early convent-school girlhood in Manila, like it was a lifeline.

She sat rigidly in a plastic chair bolted up against the wall. In front of her, a young man sporting a Sacramento police badge was frowning down at the paper-piled reception desk. He had taken her name after Officer Soto brought her in, shielding her from the TV crews decamped there. The reporters' questions came so quickly she couldn't have answered them even if she wanted to—but she didn't want to.

"Is it true that you found the sheep?"

"How much blood was there?"

After a reporter had entered the trailer disguised as a postman, Officer Soto locked the front door and seized a bottle of neon-yellow cleaning spray. Florentina watched her briskly spray the window, creating the smallest mudslides as the product and dust caked together and crawled down the glass. She could smell the lemon musk of industrial disinfectant. So much effort put into it, and it doesn't smell like lemons at all, she thought. After

Officer Soto taped a NO VISITORS sign onto the inside window, the reporters seemed to resign themselves to waiting, measuring out the hours with cigarettes and donuts, and then tossing the stubs and pink cartons into the stream that fed the American River behind the cottages.

The cottages consisted of two single-room trailers. This first was both a reception and an office, where suspects were charged in front of the emergency exit. Officer Soto's cubicle occupied a corner that housed the electrical closet and a hatch door to the roof. The second trailer was divided into a supply closet and holding cell. Together, the trailers served as the headquarters of the Olive Vale Police Station. The people of Olive Vale called them "the cottages" after the original building, a pinewood-and-stucco affair, had burned down after a Native man was detained for public inebriation and set himself on fire.

Florentina heard a phone crash into a receiver, and then a sigh. While the sheriff used the adjacent trailer as a press room, reporters called from around the country. Officer Soto spun out of her cubicle in a swivelling office chair. She wore the officer's uniform of starched mud-brown khaki. She stared at Florentina, not without compassion, but more with an anxious curiosity that made Florentina blush. It was here, for a moment, where Florentina was overcome with a kind of gratitude for her. She was a person, another person, and she was looking at Florentina and Florentina was staring back at her, as if both were dazzled by a kind of revelation amidst the fluorescent diamond-brightness inside the cottages: two people looking at each other in mutual astonishment.

Officer Soto. Sach Soto. Florentina remembered her as a lanky tomboy at Olive Vale High three years beforehand. Catholic, big family. Florentina couldn't see a spot of makeup on her image of Sach's teenaged face. Sach had never gone for any kind of reputation, good or bad—had graduated from Olive Vale High and then showed up in the Olive Vale police lieutenant's uniform three years later.

She remembered that Sach's father was the man who set the

original police station on fire.

"Whole pack of them sniffing around out there," Sach said, looking immediately as if she regretted saying it.

Florentina nodded slowly.

"I'm sorry that it's only Brad and myself," the young man looked up as if to correct her, but Sach swatted his protests away, "to take your statement today, Mrs Choi, but we're all there is at the moment. And Brad has got to get back downtown, where he is *desperately needed.*"

Sach stared at Florentina like she expected her to say something, like she wanted her to explain, but she didn't know how to begin. The three of them were quiet, so long that Sach coughed, although Florentina could tell it wasn't a real cough. Finally, Sach sat next to Florentina on one of the chairs. Flicking open a notepad, she looked pointedly at Chad, who promptly opened a large laptop. The green glow lit up his ponytail into a white-blonde halo. He nodded.

Sach turned to Florentina.

"Let's start from the beginning."

Florentina started to form her first complete sentence of the day, but changed her mind as she watched Chad, who flicked a paper clip off his desk, and then resumed his typing.

"Can you tell us what happened?"

Florentina closed her eyes.

"What time did you arrive at the scene?"

"Around six, like every morning," Florentina heard herself saying.

"And when did you notice that something wasn't right?"

"I heard the sheep, the sheep were yelling. But they weren't in the fields. So I followed the light, and saw them."

Florentina stopped, opening her eyes.

Sach nodded. "You walked from your car to the fields, and then to the classroom. And the door was unlocked?"

"It was already open."

"Can you describe the scene, when you opened the door?"

Florentina closed her eyes and looked at the dark.

You don't do anything I don't do, you shadow, she thought. You can pretend for a long time, but one day it all falls away and you are alone. She saw that all her life she had known this was going to happen, this moment, and that she had been afraid for a long time. But now it had grown, it had grown gigantic; it filled her and it filled the cottages and the whole world. But we carry our old ways with us. We may not want them, we may not love them, but we know them, and they linger.

"Mrs Choi, can you remember what you saw?"

The memory of pain began to run from the back of Florentina's neck, down her spine and between her hips, to her pelvis, the pain that pulled her to the ground ... *as he pinned her to the ground and steadied to slam the butt of the machete into her head, she twisted her gaze toward the forest floor dappled with raindrops and wild chicken shit, and then she came face to face with a dead goat.*

"Florentina?"

Her gaze began to accompany the buzzing of a midge around an empty can of sweet corn just as he ripped her rag-skirt, and she came to think about the confusing lives of midges. And in fact, she thought, there are important questions to be asked. About midges.

She saw Sach's face, blurry and shadowed, the outline of her profile dissolving at the edges. Officer Brad's mouth was working—bless him, he can speak, she thought distantly—but she couldn't hear him. *Could it be that those wings lack power to propel the owner to better grazing grounds, or were midges simply in need of dreams? Another question: how do midges feel toward us? And toward the can of sweet corn? Midges and their problems are not undeserving of our attention, or God's.*

The pain began from her pelvis to between her legs. The memory stemmed from girlhood, and Florentina met the memory of pain with the body of her age. She braced her arms against her abdomen as if she could protect herself from what she felt coming, to undo what had happened.

A second before his hand and the machete handle finished careening along their gentle axes to become part of her skull—like skin, like bone—she watched the midge fly into the sun flitting between the jun-

gle canopy above, and then wink and vanish like a fleck of gold in a river, like holy dust. She whispered deep inside the place where only she could touch and try—the place that whispered back that her brain was about to explode.

A clawing on her lower back running up her spine and to her shoulders—slipping from plastic onto concrete floor.

It is us who are not deserving of them.

She had been swimming in a place too black for dreams, inside the crevices between her own heartbeats. The impact of an icy drizzle on the tight skin of her face woke Florentina back into her body. Then sound.

"Señora!"

Something unravelled from her heart into her throat and then into her field of vision. The violence of sight frightened her. Colour and movement and touch.

Sach was kneeling beside her, a cup in one hand, the other outstretched, grazing Florentina's cheek with wet fingertips. As Florentina peered around, the sharpness of the dusty sunshine poking through the panelling of the trailer's walls reminded her that it was ambling toward sundown. Suddenly, the door of the trailer opened, and a lean silhouette, set against the desert sunset outside, coldly disregarded the sign in the window and the knives in Sach's glare, and took one step inside. Florentina saw fear lace itself across her daughter's brow like a veil as she took one more step inside and lowered her face to her mother's.

Bett's arms were wrapped around Florentina's shoulders as she spoke to Sach during the walk to the van parked in the Dairy Queen lot next door. The sky was banded: from ink-blue to soggy purple, to shades borrowed from flamboyant orchids and fire, and then sandblasted with a murky haze from the winter pollution that hung in the valley until May. Always a low time in Sacramento. In Olive Vale, the late afternoon's heaviness of quiet nothing-doing blanketed the town and made you peek out your window to check the world hadn't ended. Nobody walking on the sidewalk, no stray dogs poking their noses into the garbage, in the town her granddaughter had been born into.

As she turned to glance at the cottages, the rooftop looked like it was smoking. She remembered Sach's father.

Reporters came striding from the creek, flicking cigarette butts to the ground where their infinitesimal fires snuffed out beneath the gravel and white-bone dust.

"I'll call if we have any further questions," Sach said, opening the passenger door for Florentina, as if it were part of her job, and after Florentina climbed in she even gave it a small shove as if she knew that it needed an extra push.

Bett sat in the driver's seat and locked her door. One of the reporters was approaching their car. Her window was rolled down a few inches.

"You talk, you die," she said through the crack.

The man stopped before the van and put his hands up in a kind of *please, don't shoot* gesture, slinking back to follow Sach instead.

But Sach was already turned away from them. A blue-shirted reporter had pulled her aside. She barked over her shoulder, "They're *bastardos*," and carried on her conversation with the shirt.

They are, Florentina thought.

"They are," Bett muttered. She turned the key in the ignition, kicked the gas pedal, and the van lurched away.

AN ODE TO PUBERTY

Bethany Russell

Liv stood in the wings, elbows by her side to hide the growing sweat patches on her shirt. Mr Dendy, a tuft of hair poking out of his nostrils, addressed the rows of students.

"While taking time to relax, remember GCSEs are on the horizon. An exercised mind is an exam-ready mind."

The students groaned. He'd become their head of year a month before and this was only the latest catchphrase he'd tried out.

"A lazy mind does not an A* student make. Without further ado, let me introduce Olivia Fletcher. Olivia has been chosen to read her poem 'An Ode to Sunflowers'."

Mr Dendy gestured for Liv to join him. She took a deep breath. Staring down at her polished shoes, she stepped into the light.

"An Ode to Sunflowers," she said.

◆ ◆ ◆

An hour before, Liv had felt the familiar warm ooze in her spotty knickers whilst sitting with her friends in the quad. Her new best friend, Lucy, had been talking about an article her mum had made her read. It said that by the age of fourteen, the average girl was far less confident than the average boy.

"But way more intelligent!" Lucy said.

The cramps in Liv's stomach had started days before, but, as she searched through her bag under the picnic table, panic rippled from her stomach to her ears. A text went out to the friends around her.

I only have one and I need it and *Sorry, I'm out* came the texted replies.

She imagined herself on A-Hall stage later that day. Visions of blood dribbling down her legs, pooling around the floor, flashed through her mind. She moved quickly, albeit with thighs clamped together, to the murky toilets by the Tech rooms. The ceiling was covered in clumps of wet toilet paper, thrown up by truanting students.

If there had ever been a sanitary towel dispenser, there wasn't one now and, besides, Liv had spent her last pound on a chocolate slice at the bake sale.

She sat on the toilet with a dejected acceptance; spun off a long trail of scratchy toilet paper, and wound it around her knickers. She'd made the mistake once of simply folding the paper and placing it between her legs, but, when she'd stood, the toilet paper dislodged and fell out the bottom of her trousers. Luckily, only Miss Jackson had noticed. She'd quickly ushered Liv to the staff bathroom and placed a panty-liner in her hand.

Liv sat, toilet-paper-nappy forming, running over her poem. A week before, her class had been reading Keats' "Ode to a Nightingale". Liv had studied Keats at her old school; she could recite the poem from memory. But could she draw a nightingale? The next thing she knew Mrs Summers was hovering, eyeing her doodles. Any other teacher would have shouted. Mrs Summers told her to write her own poem instead. Liv showed the poem at the end of class and, without her knowing, Mrs Summers found her a slot to read at the end of term assembly, fifth period on the final Friday.

❖ ❖ ❖

On stage, Liv held her notebook, the pages quivering. She was sure people would be staring at her forearms. Why hadn't she shaved them? That's what Marcy had told her to do.

"An Ode to Sunflowers," Liv said again.

Half her year were staring at their laps, probably texting each other asking who Liv thought she was. She swallowed. Unlike most people, whose mouths dried up when they were nervous, Lives swam with saliva. On the front row, her friends were smiling

◆ ◆ ◆

During rehearsal in class, Liv's friends had looked at her with the same wide smiles. Mrs Summers gave Liv a minute nod.

"Go on," she mouthed.

Liv breathed deeply, fighting her desire to curl into a ball to stop the stabbing pains spreading across her abdomen. She felt sick, a combination of physical menstrual pain and mental terror at reading in front of her class.

He loves me, she loves me not,
The petals fall like tears.

By the second verse, Liv felt herself growing, taking up space. She lifted her chin, pushed her shoulders back, stepped her legs out. Her friends were nodding, Mrs Summers smiling, the class looking everywhere but at her. She read the final line from memory. Mrs Summers congratulated her and Liv took her seat.

"Was it okay?" Liv whispered to Lucy.

Lucy put two thumbs up.

Liv had thought her new friends were being nice out of politeness, but the niceness had lasted months so she was starting to believe them. She felt a tap on her back. She turned around but the boys behind her were etching into their table with a paperclip.

She turned away. A tap on her shoulder. She turned around. The boys were still etching into the table, but their shoulders were moving lightly.

"Problem?" Liv said, trying to pitch her voice low enough to seem authoritative.

One of the boys, Ben, looked up. Ben had a scar across his forehead from when his friend threw a knife at him in food tech. They'd been trying to see if he could catch it in his mouth. "Problem?" he said back to Liv.

She turned back to her desk.

"You were shit," he whispered.

She closed her eyes. Maybe she was shit.

The bell rang and class lined up for assembly. Liv took her place behind Harry Fairbrother and in front of Luis Figueira. She was taller than half the boys in her class. At her old school, they'd taken a photo on the first day of Year Seven. There she was, hair in a ponytail, new glasses overwhelming her face, shoes so heavily polished you could see the clouds in them. Liv had stood next to her form tutor and smiled. When the photos were shown as the school wished her good luck on her move to Cornwall, her head of year had remarked to the hall that it was hard to tell the teacher from the student. She'd stood half a foot above the other eleven-year-olds. She'd hoped it would be different in Cornwall. But on her first day here a five-foot-tall boy had called her a giraffe.

She'd called herself a giraffe this morning as she practiced in the mirror. Only, this time, it was because of the blanket of spots covering her face. She'd applied concealer and thought she looked better. In the assembly line, she pulled out a mirror and checked her face. The concealer had dried and formed thick flakes around each spot. She hoped the other students wouldn't notice; she'd be too far away on the stage. Maybe the stage lights would hide the spots.

◆ ◆ ◆

Mr Dendy stepped towards the podium.

"We have another child to read before the bell goes. Olivia," he said.

Ben smirked. She felt a knife stab into her aching calf. She stopped herself from yelping and let out a noise like a balloon deflating. Her mum had told her the pains would stop, usually by sixteen, but Liv didn't want to be any taller than she was now. What's the point of growing pains when you don't want to grow? As fifty pairs of eyes stared at her, and fifty pretended she didn't exist, Liv suddenly wanted to take up less space. She wished her hips would shrink, her stomach would suck in, her arms would get smaller. Slowly, the attentive eyes gave up and looked down at their laps too.

"An—An Ode to—"

Her heart was beating fast, she felt hot, she felt naked. She looked at her notebook and flipped back a few pages.

"Olivia," Mr Dendy whispered.

She looked out at the hall. Mrs Summers was smiling.

"An Ode", Liv said brightly, "to Puberty."

Mrs Summers stopped smiling. She was right at the back, but Liv could tell she was frowning.

"What?" Mr Dendy said.

Liv recited.

> *My emotions won't stay still.*
> *As I move, my body moves,*
> *And it doesn't move like it did before.*
> *I tell myself stay still.*
> *Maybe then the pain will stop.*

The smiles of her friends in the front row grew. Liv looked down at words written only days before, written as she hid under her duvet with a hot water bottle clamped to her stomach.

> *As my stomach twists into knots,*

My face fills with spots.
I moisturise, medicate, bathe and meditate,
But I can't conceal
That my skin won't heal
And these scars may last a lifetime.

Liv watched as Mrs Summers' shoulders moved up and down in a chuckle. Liv glanced to her side; Mr Dendy, hands gripping his shirt sleeves, was rocking from foot to foot, his mouth so downturned that Liv had to stop herself from laughing.

I grow taller;
Knives stab into my gut.
I grow wider;
You scream slut.
  I throw volleyballs, hit tennis balls, kick footballs, run miles.

Liv looked to where the PE teachers stood by the nearest exit.

Because you said I wasn't allowed to stay still.
All the while, my knickers are filling with blood,
Because no one has a tampon.

Eyes looked up at her and Liv felt herself growing. This time though, it was her voice, reaching out to every corner of the hall. Her friends cheered.

I feel the gorge rise in my throat.
My stomach starts to bloat.
Something stabs me in the back.
My joints start to crack.
And, no, paracetamol won't help.
I grow inwards,
As you laugh at me.

Liv breathed in and let the hall settle into silence. All eyes were now on her.

*But I grow
Like a sunflower
And bloom
Like a sunflower
And shed
My petals falling to the ground
Knowing that
This,
Bleeding,
Is my life now
For thirty – forty? – years.*

Liv shut her notebook. She turned to Mr Dendy and held out her hand. He shook it, his mouth agape. She couldn't wait to see how he followed that. She walked down the steps from the stage and looked out at the rows of wide eyes. Ben elbowed the boy next to him and started to whisper. Liv glared at him. He closed his mouth. She took her seat next to her friends and smiled.

6. PLACES I HAVE LOVED

THE FIRST FOOTING

Rosie Clemo

Mrs Edwards scraped a nail against the windowsill and sighed. She'd scrubbed it only weeks ago, but the mottled wood had bucked and bloomed in the heat. The tree was wilting too, a bushy, dark thing stuck in the corner, placed after she had received a letter from her sister.

> *We do not entirely agree with inviting a tree into one's home. But one trusts in Queen Victoria. I enclose a print of Her Majesty's Christmas for your instruction.*

Her sons had taken the picture into the forest and returned with this tree, with all the fanfare of a hunt. Adorned with sprigs of red pōhutukawa flowers and candlelight, it had enchanted the children, but now it wept sap and shed leaves. We are both in silent protest of this custom, Mrs Edwards thought.

She swept a few sand flies off the sill, avoiding the eyes of Her Majesty, whose portrait hung above the fireplace. They'd decorated the hearth with samplers of her needle class, designed to help the daughters of the Missionary Station learn basic stitch. Her daughter Maria had done a fine sampler, the stitching was neat but the embellishments to the border were strange, swirling patterns that seemed to move in the corner of your eye. Mrs Edwards had never seen the like of it before, and Maria should not have either.

She bent to the grate, cold since October and full of Paua shells from the beach, when she heard a scream. She stood up just as her second youngest charged into the room, followed by James, her second eldest.

"Run Piggy!" James bellowed, raising a stick up to his eye. "Or my musket will get you!"

Piggy, nick-named after his round cheeks, dove behind his mother's skirts.

"James! Stop that! I've not finished in here—" Before her gangly son's frame could disappear into the garden, she called him back. "The doorway? Does the Reverend think it will do?"

They had been unsure of how to solve the dilemma of the doorway. Traditionally, as the clock struck midnight tonight, the Edwards' front door would be opened to let out the old year and welcome the new, and they would be visited by friends bearing glad tidings for a felicitous year ahead. It was imperative a man took the first footing over their threshold, with coal for their fire and bread for their bellies. If he were a good-willed stranger of handsome height and dark hair, all the better. But there were no strangers in the Missionary, just three families. And as for the knocking on their front door, the heat and sour air within the cottage had forced them to host the party in the garden.

The Reverend had the idea to make a doorway outside which the men could step through, to give candied fruit to their families.

"He's fixing the archway with flax, but it looks better." James answered. "It should be fun. Will I get to do the first footing this year?"

"Not likely, while your father lives. Go see if he needs help."

She watched her son as he ducked into the garden, swinging his stick like a dandy in Oxford Circus. Mrs Edwards smiled, and then remembered Maria. "Have you seen your sister?"

"Not since breakfast."

Mrs Edwards put a hand on her belly, feeling some knot there tighten. Beyond their fence, in the shimmering heat, she could almost see Maria walk through the long grass, her hair whipped out its pins by the sea wind. But the mirage melted, and the cicadas laughed her back into the cottage.

Maria was breathing heavily, with every inhale she felt her damp corset press against her skin. The boy's finger was hovering over the linen neckline, close enough for him to feel the fibres. He traced the embroidered flowers, never fully touching, before descending a slow line towards where her navel lay. He tapped the stiffness of her corset, a frown crumpling his brow.
"It's whale bone."
"Your dress ... is whale?" Ari asked, feeling the rise and fall of the ridges.
"From the whalers in the Bay of Islands. My father tries to convince them to come to church, but they just laugh."
Ari was staring at her again.
"It must be lonely. They often lose their boats and get marooned on the islands for years."
Ari shook his head, rocking the feather in his head band, and sat to face the sea. She followed, pushing herself up from the shingle, and watched the waves catch the sinking sun. Like holding amber to the fire, the waves were veined with silhouettes, the shadows of sea creatures, and shell.
"We make this from whale bone." Ari lifted a pendant from his neck to show her. "Matau. For fish." He hooked his finger into his mouth.
She bent to inspect the pendant. The maker had carved mesmeric patterns into the bone, capturing the arc of the surf and the whorls of a river eddy.
"It looks how water looks." She said, feeling foolish, but he smiled.
"It is a gift, a Matau. From my hapü, we live by the sea."
Maria placed the pendant back against his chest. She had moved nearer, they both knew, and as their eyes met she felt that curious sense of loss, as if she was parting with something she had never known she owned.

"A gift!" She jumped, grateful to move away. "I forgot." She searched her skirts for her pocket.

But a dark-skinned hand stopped her arm.

"No gift. I do not ..." He searched for the word, muttering a language as clipped and melodious as forest birds. "Win. I do not win a gift."

"Do you mean earned? That's ok, no one does. Today is the eve of the new year, this is our tradition, my family, my whānau." She produced a piece of paper from her pocket. "We give each other gifts to say thank you."

She placed the paper in his palm. A moment passed, until his fingers closed around it.

"Tēnā rawa atu koe."

Ari unfolded the paper and became still. It was a drawing of a Tui bird, his white collar bulbous beneath the beak.

"It is the Tui, remember? The one I said looked like a Reverend had been caught by your gods and turned into a bird for his Christian ways!" She shuffled closer, inspecting her work. "I thought I got the beak wrong, but I was quite pleased with the wings. I did a Weka for mother too, that's a joke because she hates them in the kitchen."

Ari did not speak, only the Kaka's startled cry could be heard over the forest hill.

Maria began to talk faster. "The new year is fun because we get presents and have a feast. We do the first footing. Father lets you stay up to see who will knock on your door first."

The boy tilted his head to her.

"After midnight, everyone runs to visit your house, and the first visitor brings gifts with them to bless the family. Mama says a man who is tall with dark hair and carrying riches is the best!" She laughed, but he looked solemn. "Do you ... do you not like it?"

Ari took one last look at the drawing, before carefully tucking the paper into his piu piu. He stared at her, just as the year's final sun started to slip into the sea.

"Maria."

Piggy had run away as fast as his legs could carry him, which wasn't fast at all. He happily made his way through the forest. Pulling a bun from his pocket, he slowed down as he neared his secret beach, the one between Giant's Rock and God's Arc, where the tide left treasures to discover. He crashed through the bush, frightening a Kaka from its nest, and broke through the grassy cliff overhanging the beach. The sun was just slipping into the sea, and he raised his arm against the blinding light. Below, shrouded in gold sea mist, he saw them.

Piggy dropped his bun.

Ari drew his lips from hers, taking her soul with him, she thought. Who knew what magic the Maori possessed? Perhaps she had been bewitched, for she had never shared a breath with another, nor one that filled her lungs with such lightness. It was as if she had inhaled the sun. She wondered, is this how God feels? She leant closer again, but a movement on the hill caught her eye. A round, pale face and what looked like a ball, bouncing down the rocks. She locked eyes with Piggy. Then he was gone.

"PETER!" Maria screamed.

The light was fading, but Piggy knew his way to the meadow. He ran through the forest, the cacophony of birdsong spurring him to go faster. How clever ma will think me, and how jealous James will be, that I found out why Maria had been so absent ... Piggy stopped to catch his breath at the edge of the field. He could see the thatch of their roof, see the smoke twist from the kitchen chimney, and hear laughter rise into the air. He spotted his mother, alone, laying the plates. He started to run again.

Night had fallen, and the table was aglow with candlelight and red faces. Smoking eucalyptus leaf hung from the posts, warding off insects and releasing a drowsy scent. The new year's doorway had been constructed over the meadow gate that separated the garden and the field beyond. The gate was flung open to let out the old year, and the Pratt girls had decorated the arch with ferns and white-belled Kaihua flowers. The Reverend and Jimmie had been the subject of praise for their handiwork. Even Mrs Pratt commented it was pretty enough for a May bride. Maria, whose swollen eyes were noticed only by her mother, had been called to the head of the table.

"It is almost midnight." Reverend Edwards said. "Let our sweetest voice sing us into the new year."

"Maria is too tired to sing tonight." Mrs Edwards muttered to the Reverend, "She has had an adventurous day."

"Nonsense, she has the best voice! Would you rather James sing?"

The table burst into laughter, James shouted mock protests.

"Maria," said the Reverend, waving his kerchief at her. "Sing for us."

She stepped forward, out of the bruising gaze of her mother. Her voice carried through the valley, the echo of the hills created a gentle canon to her words, and their guests looked about in wonder.

> *We too have paddled in the stream From morning sun to night But the seas between us broad have roared From auld lang syne...*

She stopped, shock on her face as she stared at the archway. Her mother and father turned, the rest of their table peered around. There Ari stood, bare chest, in his skirted Piu Piu, cupping a cloth bag in his hands.

"A gift, Maria. For your whānau." He stepped through the gate.

THE DOCTOR'S HOUSE

Anna Colvicchi

Alfie and I met many summers ago. I remember perfectly what he was talking about the first time I saw him, at lunch in a little restaurant in San Teo, a small village on the way from our family's country house to the Italian Adriatic coast.

"German has its own musicality, you know? German is not a terrible language at all," he was saying to Enrico Fattori, who was sitting next to him.

I had never seen him before, which I thought was unusual. Everyone knew everybody at those lunches. My sister Silvia and I had known Enrico Fattori since the age of four, when he played with us in the garden of our country house. Now he had acne and, according to my sister, his breath smelled like cheese. During those lunches, everyone used to sit in the same spot: an unspoken rule that no one dared to break. The Grown-ups – who decided when you were grown enough to sit with them? I still don't know – always took the right-hand side of the table. The Kids – my sister, me, our friends Nick and Elena, but also our small cousins and younger children – sat on the other side. For the whole lunch, I had been too shy to sustain his gaze.

"The new guy is checking you out, Anita," said my sister. "Enrico Fattori is giving me that look again, I think he's trying to wink. I really need air."

The little restaurant was busy and smelled of *ragù sauce* and grilled meat. My dad was discussing politics with our neighbour, a retired soldier; my sister's friend Nick was asking for his third plate of pasta; my cousin Diana was asleep in her mother's arms.

"Where are you going?" I stretched my arm to grab my sister's elbow. She couldn't leave me, not now. I wasn't ready to sustain a conversation with the new guy.

Too late. Silvia shifted out of the door, and Alfie had left Enrico Fattori to talk to me.

"Can I sit here?" he asked. It clearly was a rhetorical question, since he had already taken my sister's seat. His eyes were the colour of hazels, there was something reassuring about them. I should have known that most of the troubles start with the words *can I sit here?*

Alfie and Nick never liked each other. During lunch in San Teo, when I first met Alfie, the two of them didn't talk. I could see Nick glancing from time to time when Alfie was too busy talking about German literature with Enrico Fattori to realise it; Nick would discuss the new Avengers film with my sister, and Alfie would give them a sideways look, trying to grasp what they were saying over the chatter of the restaurant.

Before Alfie made his first appearance at that family lunch, Nick was the centre of attention. He was effortlessly funny and unconventionally beautiful; the kind of beauty you need to get used to before admitting you like it. My sister and him, both blonde and fair skinned, were so inseparable people mistook them for siblings. Sometimes I had to specify that she was my sister and that I had not been adopted and no, Nick was not our brother. Alfie, so different from any of us, had an air of moral superiority about him.

I felt responsible for Alfie's entrance into our close group of summer friends, and for the fact that Nick and he never got on.

We really were a close group back then: my sister, me, Nick and Elena. She was three years older than me and I looked at her like the older sister I'd never had. She had brown hair, straight like spaghetti, and was always more tanned than the rest of us.

After lunch Elena and I were laying on the grass when Alfie came and talked to me. "I want to get as tanned as you," I was telling Elena, even though I knew that at the end of the summer I would still look like a mozzarella.

"Anita." I could see his dark silhouette against the sun. "I need to go home."

"Do you?" I didn't know what to say.

"I'll see you, I mean I'll see *you guys* around tonight?"

His tone seemed not to include the possibility of a negative answer.

At night, we liked to walk down to the river. My dad was against our night walks and now I can see his point: the path to the edge of the river was steep and the stones were slippery. My mum was more flexible. She would touch my dad's elbow, saying he was being too fussy and that we could go, but I must look after my sister and come back at ten.

That summer was for me, Nick and Alfie, the summer we turned fifteen. We felt unstoppable. There were no rules we couldn't break. Nick was the most fearless of the group, and my sister would follow him everywhere without questioning. I was more timorous, something that made me feel even more distant from the connection they shared.

That night, Alfie came with us. On the path to the river, he touched my hand slightly, pretending he wasn't doing it on purpose.

"Why is he here?" Nick whispered to me, as soon as we reached the bridge and were about to step down the narrow cement staircase that took us to the edge of the river.

I realised Nick was upset. He was not the centre of attention anymore, at least not for me. We lingered on the bridge, listening to the sound of the river behind us. "Why would you care? He enjoys our company."

"Your company. Anyway, you could ask Silvia and me next

time."

I looked at him in the dark. "That's only because you feel left aside."

"I don't know what you're talking about," Nick replied, not looking me in the eye.

"Nick?" my sister called, "Do you want to go first?"

The staircase was nestled between two big rocks, covered in moss, and the steps were slippery, so one of us had to go first, to help the others to step down.

"I'll go first if you want," Alfie said and before Nick could say a word, he was getting down, his hands on the rocks to support himself.

"Wait! I'm right behind you!" Nick started going down to the river behind him. I could feel my sister's eyes on me but decided not to say anything and for the first time I descended to the river before her, right behind the boys. Alfie offered me his hand and, when I almost tripped on a stone, his hand squeezed my elbow and I felt safe. On the edge of the river the silence was unreal. I could only hear the water gurgling and the sound of the wind through the leaves. Until Alfie decided to help my sister to go down the staircase, instead of letting Nick do it.

"Nick? It's dark, I can't see much," I heard her saying.

"It's Alfie. Come down and hold on to me, don't be scared."

It sounded patronising. I'd never heard anyone talking to my sister that way before. Everyone knew how brave and reckless she was. As a child, she was not afraid of climbing trees or playing with stray dogs.

"She's not scared, what the hell are you thinking?" Nick said, then whispered *idiot* but Alfie heard it, because he asked Nick to repeat it once more.

I could see their silhouettes in the dark, at the bottom of the staircase. They seemed to have forgotten me and my sister.

"Who do you think you are? Go back talking about your beloved German literature and leave us alone." I had never heard that tone from Nick, harsh and cold.

"Guys?" I called. "Silvia is waiting to come down, you might help her?" But they didn't seem to have heard me.

"Do you believe you are better?" Alfie whispered and his voice was calm. I guess that's what made Nick angrier. Alfie stepped closer and grabbed a strand of his curly hair. "Get an haircut."

Nick pushed him. "Get off me," he shouted. I wasn't sure if I was witnessing it for real or if I was dreaming.

"Anita? Nick? What's happening?" I heard my sister saying from up the staircase. No one replied.

"Stop it!" I grabbed Nick's t-shirt and pulled it, trying to separate them.

To resist my pull, Nick stepped forward and pushed Alfie closer to the edge of the river.

My fingertips started hurting and my palm was sweaty. I left the grip. "Nick! Why are you behaving like an idiot?" I shouted.

Nick lost his balance moving his right foot onto a slippery stone. I saw him falling, dragging Alfie with him.

7. AGE CANNOT WITHER US

FOR ALL TIME

P S Keynes

Shortlisted for the Felix Dennis Prize 2016

The police officer was not older than thirty, she would guess. Bright eyes peered out from a fair fringe as he scribbled unintelligible notes in his pad.

"I wouldn't mind a cup of tea." He grinned ruefully. "I've been on shift since six."

Bill was always writing. The skeletal hands were sprightly as they moved across the paper, pen scratching away. He eschewed computers. She had tried to bring him her laptop, but he had given her a withering look which sent her scuttling from the room and not returning for a week. And the pen suited him; it was feather-light in his hand. She couldn't imagine him tapping away at a keyboard. What had she been thinking?

She sighed and rose to fill the kettle. No one was really interested in him. He was just another old man who had wandered off from an old folk's home. He would turn up, eventually, wandering the rec and raging at the wind, or, *don't think it*, dredged from a muddy death in the Avon. He could not have vanished into thin air. Could he?

She placed the steaming mug in front of the PC and watched as he flicked through his notes: useless all. He caught her staring and chanced a question: "How do you think he got out?"

She shrugged. "The residents can come and go as they please. They have keys and are not obliged to tell us where they are going. This is not a prison. He had every right to leave."

But he should have come back.

The constable made his excuses eventually and promising publicity on social media. It was hopeless, but she nodded as if satisfied and handed over the photograph she had of Bill, clutching a pint with a serious look on his face. She hoped she would get it back; it was her only one.

"Was that the policeman?" Mrs Jonson waddled in, shopping bag over her arm. "I'm surprised they came out at all. My neighbour got burgled and it took them twelve hours to come out to her. Can you imagine?"

She passed no comment, instead allowing her mind to wander back over his worn hands, veins like ropes, age spots blending so they looked almost tanned. Imagine if humans were like ladybirds, and you could tell their age by counting their spots. How many spots would he have?

"I must get on," Mrs Jonson gave the dirty crockery a meaningful glance. "Talking isn't doing."

She shook her head and busied herself with the cups. Wash, rinse, place on the drainer. Soon the stainless steel was covered in ubiquitous roses, machine painted onto inferior pottery. There was a time when crockery from China was a luxury. Now it was the stuff of pound shops. Perhaps it was sensible to have cheap cups in an old folks' home. They were always getting broken.

She remembered the last time she had made him a cup of tea, yesterday. He had stretched his hand out, cup delicately balanced on saucer, unable to subdue the faint rattle of china.

Smiling, she had taken the porcelain and placed it firmly on the side. Steam rose invitingly from the pot as she poured, careful to add the milk last; a simple human kindness.

She had handed back the cup with exaggerated care and he had taken it wordlessly, before turning and making his slow, creaking progress towards the high-backed chairs in the window. He had carried himself carefully erect, lean in his slippers, placing one foot in front of the other like a circus artist on a tightrope. Time had wasted him, but he had not, she thought, wasted time.

"You don't want to mind him," Mrs Jonson had rattled the crockery noisily on the tray. "His sinews have stiffened up, see? He's always been moody, mind. And he's been here longer than I have."

Back in the present, the clock in the lobby chimed loudly, and in her mind's eye she watched him twitch his head in annoyance, shaking the noise out of his ears like water.

Mrs Jonson tutted. "At least he's not here to get in a bother about that clock. He was mad as the sea, that one."

The past tense already.

"He had a go at me yesterday for hoovering. Over the sound. Said he couldn't write in that racket. Can you imagine?"

She could. She could imagine lots of things when she looked at him. Fairy bowers and blasted heaths and bloody battlefields and desert islands. She could see it all.

She paused, sud-soaked hands immersed in water, and looked up through the window. Over the road, the river snaked lazily past tourists parading up and down, snapping photographs of the statue and the theatre, wielding selfie sticks like parasols, angling them away from the sun which was struggling through the drizzle. What contempt he must feel, she thought.

"I'm off for a ciggie. You alright here, love?" Mrs Jonson was out the door before waiting for an answer. She could scuttle faster than a cockroach. Resilient, that one.

She busied herself with the set up for dinner. Peeling potatoes, dicing carrots into circles, not sticks. Just as he liked them. She was preoccupied with vegetables. She sometimes wondered if she was a vegetable herself.

It was Mrs Jonson's voice which brought her back to the present.

"What have you done?"

She looked down at the chopping board, red mingling with the white starch. The cut was deep.

"Run it under the water."

She moved to the sink and ran the tap. She could see her heartbeat quicken as more blood oozed into the stream, spot after spot. She felt no pain, only light-headed.

"Calm down."

Mrs Jonson was made of sterner stuff than her; had authority in a crisis. She breathed deeply, caught her rhythm, steadied herself. The blood slowed, and she turned off the tap, reaching for a tea towel to wrap around her finger.

"Who would have thought?" Mrs Jonson was peering into the sink with ghoulish curiosity. "All that blood for such a small wound. It's turned the water red."

Outside, the sound of a siren pierced the air and tourists scurried out of its path. Her heart caught in her throat and she had to grip the kitchen side to stop her hands from trembling.

"I think I need a lie down."

She was out of the room before Mrs Jonson could object.

Upstairs, sitting on the bed, she gazed beyond the trellised roses on the wallpaper. She saw him shuffling around the streets he had run as a boy, stopping outside the family home to see the alterations that had made it a familiar stranger. And the crowds. God, he would hate the crowds. Perhaps he would make his way outside the town and find the fields he courted in as a youth, searching for those sun-soaked eternal summers when he had surrendered his virginity and his freedom, for a short while at least. She wondered if she should go out there and start looking.

She sighed and caught her reflection in the mirror opposite. A face framed by dark hair held raven-black eyes. Mourning eyes. *Golden lads and girls all must, like chimney sweepers, come to dust.* She was being foolish; he was missing, not dead. She must not succumb to mere oblivion. Not yet.

It was twilight when Mrs Jonson poked her head round the door. "You gave me a fright, lying there in the dark. It's black as hell in here. Did you nod off?"

She attempted a conciliatory smile, which came out as a grimace. "I'll be down in a minute."

Alone once more, she roused herself and went over to the window. Outside, over the Avon, the sun was in its glorious decline, bathing the theatre and the river in a golden light. A family strolled past, the woman cradling a crying baby while her husband dragged a whining boy, over-tired from a day of sightseeing and sweets. Behind them, a teenager sighed morosely as he trudged home, eyes resolutely fixed on the pavement. From behind the theatre, a portly middle-aged gentleman strolled, swinging his umbrella like a truncheon and tutting loudly as his progress was impeded by a bespectacled pensioner, pushing a companion in a wheelchair at a snail's pace. Wrapped in a tartan blanket, it was impossible to tell if the passenger was awake—head sunk on her chest, she seemed oblivious to her surroundings. Even the oaths of the father, who had just been puked on by the baby, went unremarked.

The players in the tableau moved on, their walking shadows stretching behind them in grotesque shapes. A swan glided by, head raised, looking forward into the gathering dusk. She watched it make its steady progress down the river, illuminated by a backdrop of reds and purples as the sun sank. Her eyes remained fixed on the scene until the golden orb had sunk out of sight. And yet, the colours lingered, a reminder of the dazzling glory just moments before.

Suddenly, she realised: he was not coming back.

His echoes were still around her: his tread on the stair, the rattle of his cup on its saucer, the whisper of his words in her ear. They would continue to resonate through her, like a bell chiming long after it has been struck, but the hand that shaped the mould was gone for good.

Downstairs, Mrs Jonson was solicitous. "You don't want to

mind, love." She proffered a mug of milky tea in her nicotine-stained hand. "He'd had a good life, I'm sure; he was of an age."

No, she thought, *No, he was not.*

He was for all time.

BULLETS IN THE FACE

Cheryl Powell

Published in Storgy 2019

Guy in a pizza uniform gets on the train. His face is shot full of holes.

"Do you mind if I sit here," he says, voice high, ice-green eyes unblinking.

I move my feet.

"Not at all."

I know what he is, but good manners cost nothing.

He sits down opposite and I count the bullet holes. Seventeen, blood dried black, silver bone where flesh is torn. I look away.

We're passing that new coffee plantation, pickers working the lines twenty-four-seven, their movements synchronised, a vicious sun blistering their naked backs. It won't kill them, but they suffer same as anyone.

When I look back pizza guy is prising bullets from his face

with a stud bolt remover. He'll scar and that makes him an obvious target, but I guess he knows that. He catches me looking and I act awkward and look down. My groin is still burning from the acid; it has melted my overall, lifted the flesh. But I'll fix it when I get home.

"You okay?" I ask him. "Can I help you, at all?"

His voice is bright.

"I'm very well, thank you. No help required."

He drops a bullet into the tin. I want to console him.

"I'm sorry this has happened to you."

He's now gouging out a bullet lodged in the crease of his nose.

"It wasn't you," he says, "and I am perfectly fine."

"Even so," I persist, "it shouldn't have happened. Must hurt like hell."

"You are correct," he agrees. "It does hurt. Like hell. But it is perfectly fine. How about you?"

I glance down and register pain.

"Oh, perfectly fine," I reply.

We sit in silence for a while, the afternoon sliding into a reddish evening. I watch him extract all seventeen bullets and close his tin.

"One day they'll be legislation," I tell him. "New people will have rights. "

He looks up and I note how quickly the bullet holes are closing.

"Yes," he replies. "This is what they say."

Then the train pulls into a station and a nurse gets on. The front of her white apron is thickly bloodied. She's been knifed in the stomach. She smiles at us and finds a seat.

And, for the first time, I feel something. Outrage? Fear? I turn to pizza guy and my hands are twitching and I don't know what's gone wrong.

"Don't you get scared over what they'll do next?" I blurt.

I know my voice is suddenly too loud and I'm clutching his sleeve, and inside I'm over-heating.

"Don't you ever want to fight back, destroy them; stop all

this?"

Pizza guy smiles but his voice is brittle.

"Not at all," he says. "Everything is perfectly fine."

But, you see, it's too late. There's a split-second change in his expression, a look that passes between us. And I know what he feels. That he is just like me. Waiting.

DNR

Cheryl Powell

Published in Flash Fiction Daily 2018

She opens her chest with a kitchen knife, reaching behind her breastbone, easing out her heart: such a valiant little heart. How it gasps, shocked by the freezing air.

She holds it in her palm and, under the bright light, surveys the damage: calcified scars blackened by grief, deep cracks, utterly irreparable.

Once there were only tiny fissures, like shattered china diligently glued. She had tried so hard to heal. To accept.

Into the dark hollow, she returns her heart and stitches up her chest with twine. It won't be long now.

And, for the first time in years, she smiles.

SMOKE SPIRIT

Martin P Fuller

Published by Trinity and All Saints

She sits on a throne of springs, the sofa now transformed into a twisted tangle of metal; a semi-public display of life's art. Her body's right side is a horror film special effect; charred bone and blackened flesh.

The young police officer is thankful the smell of the partly cremated body is disguised by the acrid stench of burnt wood, fabric and paint.

It's her face which claims centre stage. The old woman, as such she once was, ravaged by time and mortal afflictions, has metamorphosed into a doll-like figure, staring at the uniformed intruders in her scorched room.

The stare emanates from the remaining unburnt eye in the half-ruined skull. Its green gaze is partly hidden by a slightly drooped eyelid, speckled with soot. Her old face is smooth now, wrinkles erased by searing flame. She smiles in a shrunken grin at what remains of her home. The doll lady lacks hair, excepting a few wisps of coiled white locks adhering to the left side of her head.

The constable attempts a professional analysis, taking notes, recording the metal hooked pole lying by her side. Globs of blackened plastic cling to its once shiny steel surface.

The senior fire officer enters the room, a mask of neutral expression.

"She was a smoker, no pun intended. Ash tray in the debris. Probably fell asleep, dropping her ciggie down the back of the cushions."

The fire officer is the ordinary in the madness of the bizarre.

> **Extract from Professor Edmund Davies' pathology report: Agnes Cardew, April 29th, 1979.**
>
> *The cadaver is that of a female aged between seventy to eighty years of age and in poor physical health. Severe arthritis in all limbs has caused deformation of hands and legs, hindering mobility and probably inducing severe pain. Packets of methotrexate and ibuprofen from the deceased's residence substantiate this premise.*
>
> *The remaining skin on the left fingers are stained with nicotine. Examination of the lungs reveals quantities of tar consistent with that of a heavy smoker. Obvious signs of smoke and heat inhalation. Stomach contents indicate she'd consumed a light meal several hours before death. Traces of plastic tubing connected to the urethra show dependency upon catheter.*
>
> *Cause of death indicated by severe burning, predominantly on the right side of the body, nearest to the seat of the fire, the flesh being incinerated, exposing bone of the right arm and hand. The facial dermis has been burnt away causing polymerisation of the sub dermal fat, creating a "doll-like" effect in the face.*
>
> *The cause of death is severe shock leading to a fatal heart attack. Death was probably not instantaneous.*

Her flat gained a reputation.

Those staying within it noticed a stench of scorched paint and wood, combined with the taste of cigarette smoke. Proud new owners decorating their home saw spots of black soot marring bright surfaces and heard racking coughing fits which echoed from the room's walls.

No supernatural coldness pervaded the residence, only a hot, claustrophobic atmosphere which refused to dissipate, even when doors and windows were fully opened. Estate agents were contacted, sale signs quickly erected, and the flat remained empty, save for its only true resident.

It was where she had lived and died, alone and in pain. It was where she was determined to stay ... forever.

8. SPRING AND PORT WINE

FOOD BANK

P S Keynes

This story has been abridged.

None of us wanted to do it. We was sitting in Plus Club when Packo told us. They call it Plus Club like it's positive, but we do it cos nothing else has worked. We don't do no other classes. Just Plus Club for two hours a day, to get us a foundation level or a vocational certificate. It all helps, according to Packo.

Anyway, when he first brought up this outreach, we was all raging.

Why should we help some lousy charity?

Because you're members of the community, said Packo. You need to get some community spirit.

We ended up doing it, anyway. We moaned, but it was no use. None of us wanted to get chucked out. We'd seen what happened to Tyler. Kicked out of Plus Club, started dealing and now it's no parole til he's forty. I saw his mum down Tesco and she was in pieces. Just stared through me at the checkouts. I don't want that for my mum and I sure don't want that for me. I want a job. My own money and a life.

So I sucked it up.

Packo told us who was going where. Dev and Jack got packed off to some old folks club. Aiden and Lou went to this homeless shelter. That left me and Ro.

Food Bank, said Packo. Helping in the warehouse. And you'd better be on your best behaviour, gents? Or it's curtains for the pair of you.

He can be a right patronising git, can Packo.

First shift I turned up early cos I walked, but Ro didn't show til five past. I watched him coming across the car park, hood up, fag hanging from his fingers. I could tell, even from that distance, he was pissed. I didn't blame him. I had better things to do with my time, too.

They called it a warehouse but it was just a Port cabin round the back of the leisure centre. It was by a load of trees, and there was these piles of leaves round the edge of the building so it looked like it was sitting on this giant brown cushion.

Ro had just reached me when the door of the Port cabin opened and this woman started walking down the slope at the front – one of those concrete ones for wheelchairs. You don't think of people in wheelchairs needing Food Banks.

The woman wore a woolly cardigan and her face had too much red on it. Lipstick and blusher. Like a kid had got into their mum's makeup. I stared then she caught my eye so I looked at my feet. Ro was doing the same.

Hello boys, she said, and her voice was all gushy and posh. You must be Simon Barnes and Connor Roebuck. I'm Marion. I can't tell you how grateful I am that you've come to help. It means the world to us.

That's what she said. *It means the world to us.*

Ro gave this sort of snort, but I don't reckon she heard it cos she didn't say anything.

I'll show you the ropes, said Marion.

Alright, I said.

We walked through this reception bit which had a counter with a kettle and mugs behind it. There was prints on the walls like someone had tried to brighten the place up but all they could afford was Poundland.

This is where we meet our clients, explained Marion. This is where they get their food parcels.

Will we see any of them?

It was the first time Ro had spoken. He had this sneer on his face. He sounded like he was disgusted.

Marion didn't seem to notice.

No, she said, we've arranged for you to come outside contact hours. I'm sure you boys would be very kind, but we need to preserve our clients' dignity. It's a humiliating experience for many of them. We try to make it as private as possible.

I don't know why Ro asked that. We'd known it already.

These people are miserable enough, Packo had said. They don't need you gawping at them.

Perhaps Ro hadn't been listening.

We stepped into the warehouse. It was stacked, floor to ceiling, with those rickety shelves you get down B&Q. There was loads of them, and they all had food on them. Packets of cereal and jars of coffee and bags of crisps and tins of beans and long-life milk. All lined up.

We give out food to nearly three hundred people a month, said Marion.

She explained what we had to do. There was food in big plastic boxes at the side of the room, from collection points round town. We had to take each item, circle its Best Before date, then put it on the right shelf in date order, with the stuff about to go off at the front.

We can't give clients items that are out of date, explained Marion. And we don't want to waste any food. Do you have any questions?

No, I said.

Ro shrugged.

I'll get you both a cup of tea and biscuits, said Marion.

And she disappeared the way we'd come.

We stood for a bit, then I took off my coat.

I suppose we'd better get started.

Ro watched me circling dates with a Sharpie, then gave one of his snorts and picked up a pen. He didn't take off his coat.

We worked in silence. Then Ro started talking.

This is a disgrace, he said.

He was staring at the labels on the baked beans. It's for wasters, man. Giving out food for free. Scroungers.

I knew what he meant. Packo said the Food Bank was for people down on their luck, but I was down on my luck most of the time and no one handed me Mars Bars for free. I needed my certificate though. I could be an apprentice at a garage if I got my certificate.

Besides, I've done worse.

Marion came in with mugs of tea and a posh sugar bowl with a spoon.

Aren't you boys doing well, she said. We're so grateful to you.

Neither of us said anything.

I love the name Connor, she said, looking straight at Ro as he piled packets of pasta onto a shelf. It sounds Celtic.

No, said Ro, not turning round. It's African. I'm an African prince, me. Helping out to do my bit for the commoners. Can't you tell?

He looked at her for the first time. Dead straight.

I'll get some biscuits, said Marion.

The next week, Ro was ten minutes late. I was sorting out tins of spaghetti, when he arrived.

Alright, I said.

He grunted. Man of few words is Ro.

Marion came in five minutes later, mugs of tea in her hand.

Four sugars for you, she said, giving Ro a wink. Not that you're not sweet enough.

Ro grunted, but when she walked out to check on something

he turned to me and said, stupid cow.

What? I said.

Patronising me.

He was standing in front of a shelf with packets of chocolate bars, the sort you pick up for 50p. The sort people buy for a Food Bank because they want to be generous but not too generous. But there was also multipacks of Mars Bars.

He grabbed one and shoved it in the inside pocket of his jacket.

I didn't say anything. I didn't want to be mixed up in it. Ro'd been in trouble with the law twice – once for vandalism and once for smoking weed outside St Joseph's Primary. He lived with his mum. Her boyfriend beat him the second time he came home in a police car. Ro came to Plus Club with this bruise over the side of his face.

I couldn't get involved in that. I needed my certificate.

I turned and started on the tinned meat. Ravioli and Spam. Stuff my mum buys when Dad hasn't had many jobs on.

There was loads of donations, so we was busy, but I kept thinking about the chocolate in Ro's jacket. I didn't like it. I barely spoke—kept my head down.

After a couple of hours, Marion came to sign our timesheets. Get you used to the world of work, Packo had said. I reckon it was just another way of checking up on us.

Thank you, said Marion in her plummy voice. I'll see you next week?

I nodded and Ro grunted. We was nearly out the door, when Marion said, Have I showed you our scales?

What? said Ro.

It occurred to me, said Marion, that I never fully explained how we work. These are our scales.

She pointed to this set of scales in the corner.

You see, she said, we run like a business. We're accountable. To our donors, to our board, to our clients. We weigh everything. All the food donations that come in, on these scales here. We log the amount in this book. When we make up food parcels, we weigh those and we log them. It all balances. It has to.

Right, said Ro.

I could hear the cereal settling in the packets around us, it went that quiet.

Is that ringing? said Marion. Sorry boys, I heard my mobile. And she disappeared into reception.

We stood there and he looked at the shelves of food.

Then he reached inside his jacket for the chocolate bars and threw them on the ground. And we went outside.

Seven days later, we was back.

I've missed you, said Marion, putting our tea down beside us. You brighten my day.

Ro had been simmering since he got there. He had a fresh bruise under his eye but I didn't say anything and neither did Marion. There's no point. There's nothing anyone can do. Ro's dad hasn't been on the scene for ages.

Ro stared at the tea, then turned to Marion.

Why do you help them? he asked.

Who? said Marion. She looked straight at him, meeting his eye.

These people, said Ro. Why don't they go get a proper job?

Lots of our clients have jobs, said Marion. But can't make ends meet. Life isn't always easy.

You wouldn't catch me using a Food Bank, said Ro. I've got self respect.

He turned, dead slow, and spat in the middle of the floor.

We stared at this globule of phlegm. Silence that seemed to stretch up to the top of the shelves, past the packets of cereal. Then, Sorry, Ro said. I've got a bit of a cold.

And the world moved on.

It's alright, said Marion, I'll get a mop.

The next week, Ro didn't turn up. Or the week after that. A month later, Packo told us he wouldn't be coming to Plus Club anymore. Mr Roebuck has chosen a different path, he said.

I kept going to the Food Bank. At first, it was cos I felt embarrassed about what Ro had done, then later, once I started my apprenticeship, it was cos I was used to it.

I got quite good at it. Marion moved me to reception. I'd process vouchers, hand out food parcels and chat to clients about services they could access. I did two hours every week.

Then, one evening, he came in. He was about fifty, with a stoop and a nose with broken veins. He handed me his voucher with a hand that shook so badly I couldn't read it til I'd got it away from him. Dean Roebuck, it read, no fixed address.

I looked at him. The same mouth, curled into a sneer. The same eyes. The same look of anger that went right through you. But there was something else, too. Something you see a lot in our clients. Shame.

And he didn't have the bruises on his face like his son.

It's alright, Mr Roebuck. I took his arm and led him to a chair. Sit down here.

He moved heavily. Thank you, he said.

I patted his hand. Can I fetch you a cup of tea while you wait?

FOR ALL TIME, DEAR FRIEND

L J McMenemy

Hello, dear friend. Come in and warm yourself by the fire. It's cold outside, and you've travelled far. Sit by this open fire. Watch as the logs crackle, crumble and cremate in the hearth, as the black smoke plumes dance majestically up towards the heavens in their stone cabin. Feel the warmth radiate through your weary bones. That's it—take your boots off. Sit down. Let the old leather envelop you. Feel its skin on your skin. Hear it creak as you settle in for the night. Drink your whiskey. Hear the ice clink against the crystal glass—that one is an heirloom, isn't it? Belonged to your granddad. I remember him. I remember him well. I remember all of your family. I remember them going back many, many generations. I know you better than you know yourself.

Settle in, dear friend and rest in this darkened room. The only light is from the fire. It plays patterns on the green silk wallpaper which covers this rather masculine room. It's been there for generations. Just like this chair. And that mahogany desk. And the frayed Turkish rug. And the bookcases displaying the collection of books, none newer than your granddad's childhood; none opened in many a year.

Settle in and I'll tell you a tale. I'll whisper it in your ear. You won't even know I'm here. It goes past your granddad's time. I mention him because you know him. You don't know the boy I'm to speak of. I know him. I've been here a long time; waiting for you.

There was a boy. He lived in this house, with his mother, and his sister. His father had passed on. His mother, overcome with grief, had raised him. Raised him to the boy he was now, aged 10. Taught him right from wrong with the back of a cane. She was harsh; she wanted the best for him. With his father gone and little money, she needed him to provide.

He was not bright; would not be able to provide. Even at that age, it could be told he would not be a diplomat, nor a gentleman, nor represent his county at parliament. He would not be a teacher. Perhaps the clergy?

His mother had other ideas. Her son would be a fine pianist; play concertos around the world; mix with the best; with kings and dukes. He would be the toast of the country; of the continent beyond it ... but he could not play.

Try as he might, he could not play. She drilled him. Shook him. Pushed his fingers along the keys. Still, he could not play. Tone deaf, dear friend! She would not have it. The thought, once there, became stuck. Her son would play.

The daughter was indulged. Was embraced. was spoiled. But the son was thrashed. Thrashed until he could no longer play, and then she would thrash him some more for not playing. Do you see what a circle we find ourselves in, dear friend? The more she thrashed, the less he could play. The less he could play, the more she thrashed. I know what you're thinking, friend – why did she not give up? This mother had become possessed. She would hear nothing more. She would think of nothing more. Her son would play.

And so her son, one day, to escape his mother, ventured to an area of the house he had never been. He was forbidden to mount the stairs, and had never questioned this. Since his father had passed, the family had been confined to the first floor. He could not face another thrashing on this day. The hour of practice chimed, and he ran. Up the stairs. Up the creaking, wooden stairs he had never before looked at. Ran. Then stood, in the middle of the floor, panting, as early daylight shone through cracks in the roof and dust played around his vision. He stood. Motionless. Eyes tightly closed. If he could see none, none could see him. Trying not to attract the attention of his mother, who he could hear calling him, and moving around below.

It was because of his perfect stillness that he felt the presence behind him; then, in front. His eyes snapped open. A figure. A man. In a hooded cloak, black velvet. A faceless man. In the hood; there was none but black.

A voice.

It asked: do you want to play?

He replied that he did not.

The voice asked: your mother wants you to play?

He replied that she did.

The voice asked: would you like to please your mother?

He replied: more than anything in the world.

The voice asked: because you want to avoid the beatings?

He could not reply.

He hung his head in shame. The voice from within, the faceless man, and the boy set upon a pact. The faceless man would help him with his talent, if the boy would promise one thing. He must promise that he would stay with the faceless man for all time.

The boy, too young to understand the concept of "for all time", agreed for the sake of the thrashings.

The voice said: then it is done.

The voice said: you are mine; anything you want you must only ask.

The voice said: I will always be with you.

And the boy was pleased. He ran downstairs, taking care to avoid his mother and her cane. He walked carefully into his music room—which was, at the time, complete with a scratched black

Silbermann piano and large window overlooking the gardens. It is now this very room we sit in, dear friend—and he stretched his fingers out in front in that tradition of pianists, and began to play.

The faceless man watched over him. And the boy played well. More than well. The boy played like a genius. His mother, hearing the piano and thinking an intruder had entered, ran to the music room. She found him there, playing Bach like a prodigy. And she ran up to him. She thrashed him.

The boy asked: what was that for? I am playing well, mama!

She said: because you should've been playing like that all these years!

And so the relationship continued. The faceless man would make the boy play better. And still it was not enough for his mother.

The faceless man would bring a noted European talent finder, who proclaimed the boy the best he'd heard and asked if he could take him to play at Court. And still it was not enough for the mother. I have said, dear friend, that she was a woman possessed. She could not hear the genius in the boy's playing. Still she thought it not good enough. She favoured the daughter over the son.

Months into the arrangement, the boy began to wish away his sister. And the faceless man made it so. His sister contracted the consumption. And died. The mother was in hysterics again, and she thrashed the boy more. She still was not satisfied with his prodigious playing. She had him playing twelve hours a day to improve. She had him up before the sun and playing well into the night.

She became convinced that if he could not hear, could merely read and move his fingers, that he would play better. She burned his ears. Then, convinced if he could not see, he would feel the music; he would play better. She gouged out his eyes.

Still the faceless man watched over him. And did not intervene. The pact was done, and he made the boy play better. Deaf and blind, the boy began to wish away his mama. He did not know why this had not come upon him before, but he knew with certainty one thing: his mama gone, he would surely not have to play. And the faceless man heard this wish. It took weeks, but it did happen. Another day came when the boy could take no more. He was up before dawn to play. His mother was thrashing his fingers as they ran along the keys, black and white; shouting that he was not doing it right. Of course, he could not hear her shouting, only feel her thrashing. And that told him where she was. The faceless man gave him strength. The boy reached up and grabbed her by the neck. He placed his mama's head among the piano's wires and hammers, and slammed it repeatedly.

He broke her neck. She had gouged his eyes, so he did not see the blood. She had burned his ears, so he did not hear her screams, nor the snap of her neck as it came away from her spine, nor her dying breath.

The deed done, he continued to play. And the faceless man continued to watch over him.

For many years, and many generations, those walking these moorlands, walking past these walls and gardens, would hear the strains of Bach echo. The boy was at his piano; his mother decomposing alongside him; the faceless man watching over him.

Of course, those outside did not know any of that, nor what had happened between these walls. The family was forgotten, the years passed on. And the boy continued to play. He did not age. He had promised the faceless man he would stay with him for all time—exactly as he was.

He would pass eternity in the hell he had been trying to avoid —playing piano from dawn till dusk, playing well, and still not pleasing his mother. Oh yes, he could feel her there. He could not see her, but he knew she was there. In his head, she was telling him faster, louder, slower, pianissimo. She was there, with the faceless man, in the music room, listening to him play. For all time.

And so, dear friend, we come to present day. Your family has been attached to this house for centuries—did you know? I fear you did not. You only inherited it from your dear old granddad. Yes, I knew him. I knew them all. Watched them be born, live and die. Every member of your family. Until they moved away, that is. Your grandmamma could not handle the playing. The old music room had long been boarded up. The house had been found abandoned by a relative who came to visit. And, this house being larger than theirs, they moved in.

And so began the constant stream of people. Generations won and lost, all through these walls. But never these particular walls. No, this room was off limits. Until you arrived.

The others; they couldn't be in here. They knew the story; knew what had happened; felt what had happened. They saw the books be thrown across the room; saw the glasses drop; saw the fires light and unlight.

They heard the playing. My playing. Yes, dear friend. I'm here. Still playing from dawn till dusk. And I don't like to be interrupted. I wish you'd stayed away. The others did.

But here, let me play for you. I'll play some Bach, and you can listen. It's really very good. Mama doesn't think so, do you mama? She's been here, and will be here, with me for all time. Listening to my playing. Did you know Mr Haydn complimented me on my playing? But mama would not let me go with him, would you mama?

Dear friend. Sit down and rest. Warm yourself by the fire. It's cold outside, and you've travelled far. Settle in and rest in this darkened room. The only light is coming from the fire, and it plays patterns on the green silk wallpaper which covers this rather masculine room. It will soothe you as I play.

Meet my old master, dear friend. Do not let his faceless nature disturb you. Look into his darkness. It will make the end come sooner...

9. DREAMS AND NIGHTMARES

ONE DAY

Costanza Casati

One day
    we will drift apart and fall
    into other people's arms
into other people's lives
and lie
just like we lie now
my head on your shoulder
your sleep restless.
Can we feel nostalgia for the future?

THE CRAVING

Cheryl Powell

Published by Coffin Bell

It is exquisite to crave. And we are no strangers to craving. We have stalked so many other superstars; craving doesn't faze us. It's the nature of obsession, after all.

High on the ledge, we know exactly how to flatten our bodies, shift our feet, focus on the slew of stars above us. And there is nothing we will not do to see this superstar, to look into her legendary eyes, witness their sorcery.

We check our phones, monitoring for updates. We scroll through her night's tweets, the glitter and gush of her latest premiere: Helvetica wide-mouthed on the red carpet, paparazzi eyes flirting with the cameras, clinging to Viktor. Darlink Viktor.

Out on the ledge, the night breeze loops around our hot bodies, disturbing our hair, slipping over our lycra-slick bodies. It is nearly time. And oh, how we crave. Below, the streets are growing dark and treacly, a city folding in on itself; hunkering down its fashionable cargo. We yearn.

Helvetica has checked into the Boiler-Room suite alone, unaware that we crowd and cling at the window. And wait.

She has done well. Born in the gutter, once a porn star, she has clawed her way to fame and ludicrous wealth. We love her for that. She isn't even beautiful. If it were not for those enigmatic eyes, she'd be quite mundane. But they are the eyes of a goddess.

From the far end of the ledge, we can see through the unshuttered window: a wide-angled space; bare, whitewashed and high-ceilinged; the bed off centre, its white pillows and silken sheets stacked and pristine, the small hours as yet unwritten.

She is working the phone with her thumbs, tweeting syrupy goodnights to her followers, and we instantly pick up the message, our stomachs swilling with vicious longing.

Now she is undressing, vipering out of her black silk dress: the china-plate smoothness of her stomach, the bevel of her pubic bone, breasts still new from their wrapper. She wears no jewellery, accenting her one defining feature: her eyes. So green, so poisonous. How they haunt us.

She turns down the lights and her pupils bloomed like dark suns. She stands naked, and we lean in. She is before a smooth black box on the dressing table, lifting the lid reverently, sleek fingers, cadaver nail polish. The box is empty.

We wait, drinking her in, and she takes deep breaths, removes her contact lenses, squeezing them out one at a time. But we see at once, they are too large for lenses; they are vitreous and slippery and she places them carefully inside the box and closes the lid.

Out on the ledge, our hearts break loose and hammer in our chests. She turns to the window, a crease in her forehead, but we hold still, as one, a dark knotted thing, transfixed by the shock of her eyeless sockets. And then she turns and walks, arms out, feeling her way to the bed. We watch how she gropes, her body sagging slightly, buttocks lop-sided as she stumbles a little. Never have we loved her more.

Helvetica takes Rohypnol's to sleep. We know this and we wait. Within minutes she is unmoving. We ease onto the windowsill, flat-palmed, cheeks pressing to glass. We lift the sash and climb in.

She is curled up on top of the bed, like a question mark in a wordless void, and we stare down and ponder: *eyeless woman in white room*.

We move to the black box, one of us opens it, the rest of us crowd. There they are: the eyes, cradled upon red velvet. Her eyes. Although detached from their cranial nerves, they are still alert and gazing, their corneas sucking in what little light there is, the pupils pools of dark water. They know we are there: they look straight into our faces. Then, one winks, just a flicker, as a camera shutter captures an image at a fraction of a second. And we imagine a small inverted picture of ourselves, suspended at the back of the retina, ready for her brain to process us. It sends silvery thrills through our bodies.

Then, one of us raises a hand, and the eyes roll upwards, following the movement. We falter. The eyes unnerve us, those great liquid orbs, almost black, and we can feel the heat, red-hot, the optic nerves snapping and sparking. Such pain: how those eyes must burn her. We are all forever burning, aren't we?

We close the lid, knowing the eyes will smoulder into the darkness, waiting for her to claim them again, for her to master the agony for another day.

We climb onto the bed beside her, close enough to see the smoke roiling in her burnt sockets, close enough to see the tiny scars threaded around her breasts, eyes and lips, and close enough to see somebody else's voluptuous hair glued in strings next to her own.

One of us slides the phone loose from her grip and holds it above us and we move closer. She will be anaesthetised for hours yet, and we put our cheeks next to hers. She does not move, does not even flinch when the flash goes off and our image flips onto the screen. She is totally unaware that we lean over her, over the two smoking voids, and kiss her on the lips, all of us. One of us uploads the image and presses *post*.

The minders outside her door pick up the tweet and are lumbering in, talking into their sleeves, and that makes us smile. We know we must leave quickly, though not without her eyes. Flinging open the box, one of us snatches them up, recoiling under their intense heat, all of us feeling our skin blister.

Then, we are back on the ledge, the breeze stronger now, tearing up the sky, streets sprawling a mile below like fabulous detritus. A light is on in another penthouse, another maimed celebrity within our reach. And this how it always goes, this insatiable need. This craving.

SNAP ALLEY

Martin P Fuller

Previously published by Sirens Call e-magazine

No one enters Snap Alley. Not anyone ... ever.
Everybody knows this. It's a canticle reciting in your head when you're near its narrow throat and its warnings scream in your mind, silent as falling snowflakes, but there nevertheless; mentally blinding you to its presence. Its only known entrance is on Harper Street; an oblong maw squeezed between high walls of red brick, the colour of dried blood. An urban canyon between derelict warehouses, its broken cobbled path winding out of sight, hiding around future corners. Devoid of bins or dumpsters, doors or gates. There are no streetlamps to reveal its inner gloom and even growling dogs, creeping cats and worried rats, avoid its open gloomy mouth.

Nothing enters Snap Alley. Ever.

Until one autumn night ...

"Jimmy Fast Blade", savage with fists of gold rings, the ruthless administrator of shark bite loans and Duke of the street's drugs trade. He was the "Cut Man", meanest of the mean. Take your pick of the honorific titles whispered softly by crony and desperate customer alike.

Jimmy knew about Snap Alley. Knew it wasn't quite right. And yet ...

He'd dared to dream a scheme about the brick squeezed track, unused by a cowed community already fearful of home-grown human nightmares. He challenged the caution his cruel brain dispensed, desiring places of concealment for deals and merchandise. A place where even cops avoided; a perfect H.Q for an up-and-coming entrepreneur ... if he can face down his fears.

Jimmy trains his eyes to look straight into the heart of the alley's shadows, building up a resistance to the dire feelings it radiates. He swears he'll conquer the urban gorge, tread its crazed stone flagstones; discover its secrets.

How unfortunate his plans are suddenly overturned by events in his busy commercial life.

A rival emerges bringing issues over territory, attempting an aggressive takeover on Jimmy's lucrative businesses. The competitor faces Jimmy's quick blade at high mid-night, blood flows and a scream escapes into the dark. Suddenly, no more rival to the kingdom's crown and Jimmy's reputation upheld to the max. All's cool except for someone's ratted him out. Crimson stains on his designer clothing and usurper's blood splashed on his skin are a forensic scientists' dream.

Problem. Cops searching the streets. His crew split, crawling under stones to escape from searching blue lights and the buzz sound of a cop helicopter. The Law knows his usual haunts, his safe places no longer safe. He needs another refuge where he can ditch the bloodied blade, clean up, wait out the storm of blue justice blowing around town. A sanctuary to think in, contact his sycophantic gang; arrange fresh clothing and solid alibi, avoiding the beckoning vision of hard prison time.

There's only one place.

A hide-and-seek half hour of street corners, doorways and crawling behind fences. Cops with dogs, tracking his blood smell, his sweat trail.

Snap Alley emerges, its walled gloom promising safety. He enters, the alley embracing him in its clammy cold comfort.

Jimmy wears the darkness like a shroud, breathing it in as it covers his existence. He moves forwards, looking back in frightened glances, admitting he's scared. Snap's entrance is framed in neighbourhood lights, wails of sirens giving music to the night.

Hesitant steps forward, the road glow from his own world dimming; sound becoming deadened. A turn of the walls robs him of his streets, the world where he dreamed of kingship.

Jimmy grasps his bloodied blade and our vicious Orpheus begins his journey to the underworld, blind in the black silent nothingness, desperation pushing him deeper into the alley. The taste of the streets fades in his mouth, senses becoming redundant in the utter night in this man-made ravine. He grabs a gaze upwards, hoping for stars or a moonshine blessed sky, but only darkness presses down, like the walls are bending over the gap, cutting away the cosmos.

Limited choices urge him on. The bricks change to black stone, bleeding out a fungi glow of tomb green fluorescence. He shuffles in the dead light across cobbles layered in slimy lichen.

His nerve decays, chest heaves, heart flips, groping his way along walls narrowing to a choke point. Fingers feel rock and old mortar. He's a shambling lost figure, tripping on uneven edges, searching for hope.

Impish thoughts sneer at his reason, whispering *What if it's got no exit?*

Time melts away leaving him isolated in the dark. The walls rescind their pus-coloured light and flat pack terror assembles itself in poor Jimmy's brain. He feels shapes lurking in the-no-light, moving slivers of ... something.

He wonders at his madness, trying to reason. *Cops must be gone by now, turn back.*

His brutal intelligence donates an idea.

He fumbles for one of his phones. Not the business phone he

does the dealing on; a phone for directing violence on those who cross him. The cops could trace it.

No. Best to use the other phone; his friendly phone; the one he uses to ring his mother, waking her from her failed sobriety; the sexy phone used to summon his deadhead girlfriend who'll do anything for her fix. He yearns for the screen's brightness, a beacon guiding him from the confines of the alley.

Cold fingers fumble in panic across the switch. The alley is pierced by white light and jolly notes of the mobiles awakening.

Clarity is granted on his surroundings, and a final horrific revelation.

The alley is indeed a dead end in all sorts of ways, its perpetual resident revealed in the limelight; a thing which feeds on those foolish, desperate and delicious enough to trespass in its domain built of stone and brick. It smiles a smile which perhaps only Jimmy's stiletto blade could appreciate.

Poor Jimmy's screams turn to mumbled gurgles from a blood-filled throat. The friendly phone falls, shattering on the unfriendly hard surface of an unreal reality.

No one enters Snap Alley and certainly, no one ever, ever, comes out.

CIRCLES

Patrick Cronin-Coltsmann

She had been walking to the house from the bus stop for fifteen minutes and was nearly at the door. It was only a couple hundred metres but she had been determined to draw it out as long as possible. That door, what it meant, what it held behind it, was terrifying. But she knew she must reach it, inevitably. She wouldn't be able to stomach herself if she turned back. Not again. A tenuous spark of resolve held in her mind for just a fraction of a second, before it was dwarfed and subsumed by the continuous rolling waves of dread she waded through.

A gate. She allowed herself a moment's hesitation, bathed calm, without onus, internal or external. For a fleeting second, she was free. She breathed. And the moment was already over, as if it had never even existed, and she felt her feet drag and lurch beneath her towards the towering door.

Its presence was overwhelming. Noise and light effervesced from its cracks, drowning her in their flow. Her pace slackened further, such that she was barely even moving. But move she must. The dread moment, the pinnacle of her horror had arrived. The insurmountable obstacle that only held further unknowable dread behind it. She knocked on the door and it opened wide before her. Fiery tendrils reached out from the brightness within and coiled around her. They seared against her skin and dragged her through the tall portal into the blinding incandescence.

Pyres burned in every corner, each manned by a different gruesome demon, red skinned, cloven hooved and curling horned. They sneered and jibed at her, beckoned her with one arm while gripping blood tipped pitchforks in the other. The floor beneath her blistered her feet. Imps clambered over her, tugging and nipping at her skin with long claws and fine teeth. Spinning around, she saw no exit. Everywhere was blocked by walls of burning flame or jeering devils. They advanced upon her, faces contorted into horrific smiles. As they closed about her, tridents pressing into her skin, drawing blood and pain, she saw a gap. If she pressed further into the throng she may get to it. Spears stabbed deeper into her, gouging her flesh and drenching the floor in her blood. She broke through the crowd and sprinted for the white beyond the doorway, as she got closer she felt her skin bubble and boil in the heat. She threw herself into the cool bliss of the adjacent room.

The kitchen, cheap white linoleum upon the floor and blank counter surfaces, was open. She staggered to the tap and drank straight from it. She'd made it here, that was what was important; she just needed to survive from there on in. It was cold in there, a stiff breeze blew in from a second open door leading to an inky blackness. To busy herself, she went from cabinet to cabinet, feigning a search for a glass.

"There are glasses on the drying rack just there," a familiar voice called out from behind her.

She spun, caught in the act. "Oh. I didn't see them."

"I'm glad you made it. Hey, it's a bit quieter out back, there are a few of us in the garden. C'mon, I'll introduce you."

"No, it's ..."

It was already too late as he stepped through the black gateway and was swallowed by the darkness. She would have to follow, there was no other option.

She walked up to the blank space and stared into the void. The empty chasm tugged at her soul. A million miles away, she thought she could make out small lights, glowing and bobbing in the abyss. She grew dizzy and steadied herself against the wall before the gateway, her breaths grew quick and short. In a single decisive action she plunged herself into the emptiness and was swallowed by it. Oblivion surrounded her and ate away at her edges. Her being dissolved in the great nihility.

Then, at the end of eternity, she opened her eyes.

She looked at herself in the bathroom mirror. Her face was blanched and her eyes were sunken. She was covered in a slick film of cold sweat and she felt warm saliva at the back of her throat. She looked at her watch. An hour had passed. Surely that was enough? She splashed her face; sat and tried to breathe deeply and slowly. The worst was over and she could escape. She studied magazines and shampoo bottles to let time pass.

Voices and the laughter came through the walls and her heart wrenched anew; her stomach again turned in on itself. She pressed her hands against her ears to block it out. She drew deeper and deeper breaths. Get up, open the door and act normally and get out of there. She could do it. She slowly lifted herself from her seat, staggered forward and reached for the handle. She turned the lock underneath, pushed the door open and braved the storm.

It whipped around her and lacerated her skin. The wind beat at her ears and filled them with its shrill howling. It pushed against her to deny a chance at release. She squinted and brought her hand up to shield her eyes. Tears began to streak down the sides of her face, but ultimately were drowned amidst the torrent of the tempest.

One foot after another she made her steady progress. Hailstones began to pelt her, starting small but growing larger and larger until each was a blow strong enough to make her stumble. Though her stride faltered, she continued.

Through a break in the squall she glimpsed the side door to the alleyway between the houses. So close. A sudden burst threatened her progress but she hunkered by the wall. A few more steps. She outstretched her arm and felt the cold metal against her hand. She mustered everything she had, every part of her ached and strained but she with one final effort, she broke through.

She stole down the alley and out into the road; gave a furtive look back at the house and fled into the night.

10.MEET THE WRITERS

BIOS

Ankit Agrawal

Ankit is a qualified chemical engineer who works as a data analyst. Ankit's blogs cover a range of topics from life experiences of a creative mind confined to a wheelchair to questions related to democracy, philosophy and the world in general. i.ankit.agarwal@me.com

M. Rene Bradshaw

M. Rene Bradshaw grew up in Filipino kitchens in California and lives in Norwich. She is an international project manager in the tech industry and a PhD student in Creative and Critical Writing at UEA. Her writing has appeared in the TLS, Litro, The London Magazine and elsewhere. The critical component of her PhD focuses on food, media and power. mrenebradshaw@com

Costanza Casati

Costanza is a twenty-five-year-old writer, screenwriter and freelance journalist. Her feminist dystopian novel, *The President Show,* is available on Amazon. She writes contemporary, historical and dystopian fiction and is currently at work on a novel on the life of Greek heroine Clytemnestra. Her short stories in the anthology are inspired by her mother's childhood in Italy. costanza.casati1@gmail.com

Rosie Clemo

Rosie is a London-based writer. Having finished her Masters in Writing at Warwick in 2019, she returned to work in education as a university outreach officer. She is currently working on her debut novel.
rosieandwriting@gmail.com

Anna Colvicchi

Born and raised in Rome, Italy, Anna is a journalist and writer based in Lancashire, where she works for a local newspaper. A graduate of the University of Warwick's Writing Programme, she writes about climate, politics, food and gender. She also writes fiction. annamaria.colivicchi@gmail.com

Patrick Cronin-Coltsmann

Patrick is a PhD student studying astrophysics at the University of Warwick. This is not amenable to his ongoing campaign to visit as many different civilisations and underwater shipwrecks as possible, so instead he's been spending his spare time knitting and trying out writing. patrick.coltsmann@gmail.com

Thea Etnum

A multilingual writer and translator, and occasional photographer, words facilitate Thea's exploration of the world, helping to make sense, fun and art out of the human experience. Thea is looking forward to the moment she will write the last sentence of her first book. theothereden@yahoo.com

Martin P Fuller

Martin Fuller started writing five years ago by taking a local creative writing class. He loves darker fiction and comedy. He is a retired police officer dabbling in antiques and lives in Yorkshire. martin_fuller@live.co.uk

Elif Gulez

Elif is a PhD student in Literary Practice at Wrawick University. She holds an LLM degree in International Human Rights Law;and MA in English Literature and an MA in Creative Writing. She is an exophonic writer and a self-translator. Elif has just finished the writing of her first novel in English. She lives in Leamington Spa with her husband Candas, her son Can and their working cocker spaniel, Nacho. e.gulez@warwick.ac.uk

Katie Margaret Hall

A poet since childhood, Katie is a journalist, creator of the UK's first lesbian web series, and co-creator of the eccentric *Inspector Detective On Chan Tay* podcast. Shortlisted for the Lichfield Cathedral The Word poetry prize, Katie was recently announced for the 2020 Primadonna Writing Prize longlist. katie.kmhmedia@gmail.com

Elise Heath

Elise finished her undergraduate degree in English and French in 2018. She went on to study a Master's in literary translation and wrote her dissertation on translating queer feminist writing from Quebec. She is currently teaching English at the University of Burgundy. eaheath.live.co.uk

Naili Huda

Naili is currently pursuing her PhD at the University of Warwick. Although life often overwhelms her, becoming a writer has become the light in the end of her tunnel. She admires Michael Crichton's imagination, John Steinbeck's ease and Kazuo Ishiguro's ways to break hearts. vedderforeva@yahoo.com

P S Keynes

Penny has had a short story published in the Felix Dennis Prize Anthology, she was runner-up in a Faber Academy Quickfic Flash Fiction Award, and she recently had a story shortlisted for the Bridport Prize. She's represented by Becky Bagnell at The Lindsay Literary Agency. penny@penchard.co.uk

L J McMenemy

Lauren is an Australian-born, London-dwelling writer of the spooky, the creepy and the quirky. She has been published in several anthologies, is co-chair of Sutton Writers, and is working on her debut novel, a gothic-influenced horror set in the Australian outback. wherelaurenwrites.com and twitter is @novicenovelist

Abigail Penny

Abigail graduated from the University of Warwick with a Master's degree in English Literature in 2019. This is her second anthology publication, with three of her poems being published in the 2017 anthology *Stairs and Whispers: D/deaf and Disabled Poets Write Back*. abigail.penny@outlook.com. Poetry instagram, https://www.instagram.com/crescentius_/

Cheryl Powell

A graduate of Warwick's MA Writing programme, Cheryl explores tragedy and absurdity. She is published in *Disturbing the Beast*, *The Mechanics Institute Review 2018*, *Reflex Fiction*, *Flash Fiction Magazine*, *Flash Flood*, *Storgy*, *Litro*, *Coffin Bell* and *Spelk*. She runs a writing group in Droitwich, Worcestershire. cheryl.powell@btinternet.com

Bethany Russell

Beth works for a theological college in a very non-creative role (think spreadsheets and KS3 maths!) but in her spare time enjoys painting, baking and, most importantly, writing. Beth completed an MA in Writing at Warwick University and is now writing her first novel.

Miloni Shah

Primarily a copywriter, in her own space, Miloni writes about families and friendship, drawing out the most ordinary aspects of a relationship in microscopic detail. milonishah27@gmail.com

Benjamin Waller

Benjamin lives in Warwick and works as a freelance writer, consultant, and occasional lecturer. He is working on a novel exploring love, loss and digital life after death, and another telling the life story of a young man with learning difficulties. benwaller@outlook.com

Cameron Yanoscik

Cameron enjoys writing about fairy tales, fantasy and the supernatural. He received his BA in Comparative Literature at the University of California, Davis and his MA in Writing at the University of Warwick in Coventry. He now calls Santa Fe, New Mexico his home. yanocam@gmail.com

TALES FROM THE ETHER

EPILOGUE

We hope you enjoyed this anthology. It was a pleasure to bring such a range of vibrant and original writing to our readers. Please check out our website to learn more about our writers and other publications.

orangepetalpress.com

ACKNOWLEDGEMENT

Thankyou to Jenny Mak and Bethany Shepherd, both of whom helped to bring this anthology to fruition. Jenny had the great idea of running a radio show to share the work of amazing writers at Warwick University, *The Writing Haunt* (thewriting-haunt.com) and beyond, and then she transformed this into a podcast during lockdown. Jenny, Beth and I co-presented *Flash Fix*- the radio show and *Flash Fix* -the podcast. Jenny did the original typesetting for the anthology and moved us forward through her energy and can do attitude. Jenny also wrote the introduction to the anthology. And of course, Beth was always there to support, support and support some more. Thankyou Jenny and Beth.

Marsaili-Editor

Printed in Great Britain
by Amazon